Women of the Bay State:

25 Massachusetts Women You Should Know

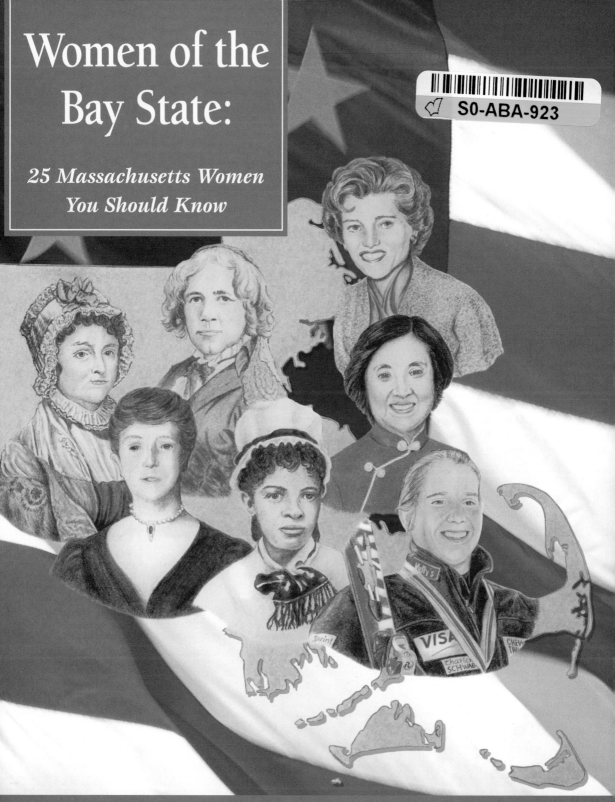

© 2009 Apprentice Shop Books, LLC • Bedford, New Hampshire

Written by Kathleen W. Deady & The Write Sisters • Illustrated by Lisa Greenleaf

Apprentice Shop Books, LLC
Bedford, New Hampshire

Text copyright ©2009

For information regarding permissions contact:
    Apprentice Shop Books, LLC
    7 Colby Court, Box 156
    Bedford, NH 03110
    www.apprenticeshopbooks.com

LIBRARY OF CONGRESS CATALOGING-IN-PUBLICATION DATA

Deady, Kathleen W.
    Women of the Bay State: 25 Massachusetts Women You Should Know by Kathleen W. Deady
    and the Write Sisters. Illustrations copyright © 2009 by Lisa Greenleaf
Summary: Profiles of 25 influential Massachusetts women. Includes bibliographies for additional research.

1. Massachusetts, Juvenile non-fiction. 2. Famous Massachusetts women. 3. Women artists—United States—Massachusetts—biography—juvenile literature. 4. Women athletes—United States—Massachusetts—biography—juvenile literature. 5. Women writers—United States—Massachusetts—biography—juvenile literature. 6. Women in public service—United States—Massachusetts—juvenile literature.

ISBN 978-09723410-5-9

Oceanic Graphic Printing, Inc.
105 Main Street
Hackensack, NJ 07601

Printed in China

On the cover: Clockwise from bottom right Laurie Stephens, Mary Mahoney, Isabella Stewart Gardner, Abigail Adams, Maria Mitchell, Eunice Shriver, Joyce Chen

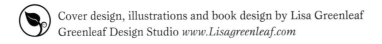 Cover design, illustrations and book design by Lisa Greenleaf
Greenleaf Design Studio *www.Lisagreenleaf.com*

15 14 13 12 11 10 9 8 7 6 5 4 3 2 1

A Timeline of Massachusetts History

1620	Pilgrims establish a colony at Plymouth, Massachusetts.
1630	Puritans start the Massachusetts Bay Colony in Boston. The Puritans have little religious tolerance.
1650	**Anne Dudley Bradstreet** publishes the first book of poems written in America.
1659	Puritans hang **Mary Dyer** for her beliefs.
1692	Salem Witch trials held in Salem. **Rebecca Nurse** is hanged as a witch.
1763	**Elizabeth Porter Phelps** begins keeping a diary that will inform future generations about the period.
1773	The Daughters of Liberty help boycott British goods.
1776	The thirteen American colonies declare independence from British rule.
	A letter written by **Abigail Adams** becomes the first to demand equal rights for women.
1831	In Boston, William Lloyd Garrison publishes the first anti-slavery newspaper.
1834	The Factory Girls Association stages a strike at the mills in Lowell, MA.
1840	**Lucretia Mott** attends an anti-slavery convention in London but male delegates vote that women cannot participate.
	Dorothea Dix is a leader in the Asylum Movement, aimed at improving conditions in mental hospitals.
1847	**Maria Mitchell** discovers a new comet.
1850	The first *national* women's rights convention held in Worcester, MA to "secure…political, legal, and social equality with men."
1861–1865	Over 160,000 Massachusetts men serve in the Civil War. Women like **Louisa May Alcott** tend the wounded.
1863	Lincoln issues the Emancipation Proclamation freeing slaves.
1870	15th amendment passes, which provides that men can vote regardless of race, color, or previous status as a slave. Suffragists continue to fight for women's voting rights.
1917	The US enters WWI. It will end in 1918.
1920	Women win the right to vote with ratification of the 19th amendment.
1925	**Edith Nourse Rogers** becomes the first woman elected to congress.
1929–1939	The Wall Street crash of 1929 marks the start of The Great Depression.
1941–1945	WWII. Women take on 'men's work' while US soldiers fight overseas.
1942	The US creates women's military branches. **Nancy H. Love** becomes the first woman to fly for the military.
1955–1968	The Civil Rights movement aims to abolish racial discrimination against African Americans.
1960	John F. Kennedy is the fourth Massachusetts man elected president of the US.
1965	Congress passes the Voting Rights Act. It bans unfair practices that keep African Americans from voting.
1966	Edward Brooks is the first African American elected to the U.S. Senate.
1965–1972	1,323 Massachusetts men and women die in the Vietnam War.
1972	Congress passes Title IX. This act allows women equal participation in federally sponsored programs. Until this time, women's participation in school sports is limited.
1974	Federal courts order the integration of Boston Public Schools.
1988	Massachusetts celebrates its bicentennial.
2004	Boston Red Sox win their first World Series in 86 years. **Laurie Stephens** is the Mono-ski overall champion.

Author/Writer Credits

"Mary Dyer: Quaker Martyr," "Lucretia Coffin Mott: Suffragette and Abolitionist," "Nancy Harkness Love: First Woman to Fly for the Military" copyright © 2009 Janet Buell

"Anne Dudley Bradstreet: America's First Poet," "Maria Mitchell: Astronomer and Educator," "Lucy Larcom: Millgirl, Teacher, Poet" "Tenley Albright: Olympic Gold Medalist and Surgeon," "Laurie Stephens: Paralympic Alpine Skier" copyright © 2009 Kathleen W. Deady

"Rebecca Towne Nurse: The Salem Witch Trials," "Isabella Stewart Gardner: Patron of the Arts," "Eunice Kennedy Shriver: Founder of the Special Olympics" copyright © 2009 Andrea Murphy

"Abigail Adams: First Lady of the United States," "Ellen Swallow Richards: America's First Woman Chemist," "Marita Bonner: Harlem Renaissance Writer" © 2009 M. Lu Major

"Elizabeth Porter Phelps: Diary Keeper," "Dorothea Dix: Friend of the Friendless," "Louisa May Alcott: Writer, Reformer, Celebrity" copyright © 2009 Sally Wilkins

"Mary Mahoney: First Black Professional Nurse," "Florence Bascom: Geologist," "Edith Nourse Rogers: First Massachusetts U.S. Representative," "Katharine Lane Weems: Sculptor," "Joyce Chen: Chef" copyright © 2009 Diane Mayr

"Edith Wharton: Writer," "Bette Davis: Actress," "Mary Bunting: Scientist and Reformer" copyright © 2009 Barbara J. Turner

Illustration & Photo Credits

Cover & pages 7, 12, 17, 27: illustrations by Lisa Greenleaf

Cover—background photo from Veer.

page 9 The Granger Collection, New York

page 19 © 2008 JupiterImages.com

page 22 Library of Congress, Prints & Photographs Divison, LC-USZ62-10016

page 24 Courtesy of the National Park Service

page 29 Porter-Phelps-Huntington Foundation, Inc., Hadley, MA, Porter-Phelps-Huntington Family Papers (Box 132, Folder 2), on deposit at Amherst College Archives and Special Collections, Amherst, MA

page 32 Library of Congress, Prints & Photographs Divison, LC-USZ62-42559

page 34 "Postcard of Lucretia Mott." Votes for Women: Selections from the National American Woman Suffrage Association Collection, 1848-1921, Library of Congress

page 37 The Granger Collection, New York

page 39 Courtesy of the Architect of the Capitol

page 42 The Schlesinger Library, Radcliffe Institute, Harvard University

page 44 Courtesy of NOAA Photo Library

page 47 Apprentice Shop Books Photo Collection

page 49 Library of Congress, Prints & Photographs Division, LC-DIG-nclc-02445

page 52 Library of Congress, Prints & Photographs Division, LC-USZ61-452

page 54 Courtesy of Wikipedia Commons

page 57 © Burstein Collection/CORBIS

page 59 Courtesy of K. G. Brown

pages 62, 64 Courtesy of MIT Museum

page 67 Courtesy of New York Public Library

page 69 Courtesy of Diane Mayr

page 72 Library of Congress, Prints & Photographs Division, LC-USZ62-29408

page 74 Yale Collection of American Literature, Beinecke Rare Book and Manuscript Library

page 77 Courtesy of the U.S. Geological Society

page 79 Sophia Smith Collection, Smith College

page 82 Library of Congress, Prints & Photographs Division, LC-DIG-npcc-15052

page 84 © Bettmann/CORBIS

pages 87 & 89 The Schlesinger Library, Radcliffe Institute, Harvard University

page 92 Katharine Ward Lane (Weems), between 1920 and 1930/ 1 photographic print: b&w; 9x6 cm. Courtesy of the Katharine Lane Weems papers, 1865-1989, Archives of American Art, Smithsonian Institution.

page 94 Courtesy of Diane Mayr.

pages 97 & 99 Popperfoto/Getty Images

page 102 The Schlesinger Library, Radcliffe Institute, Harvard University

page 104 Time & Life Pictures/Getty Images

page 107 Courtesy of National Archives

page 109 Courtesy of the U.S. National Air Force Museum

pages 112 & 114 Courtesy of the Joyce Chen Family

page 117 Courtesy of the JFK Presidential Library

page 119 Courtesy of the Hill Military Base

page 122 Time & Life Pictures/Getty Images

page 124 ©2006 Getty Images

page 127 & 129 Courtesy of the Family of Laurie Stephens

Table of Contents

— 1 —
Mary Dyer:
Quaker Martyr

by Janet Buell

Mary Dyer stood on the **gallows** with two other prisoners. The nooses tightened around their necks. Still, the three called out against Puritan leaders.

The Puritan drummers did as instructed. Each hit of the stick tried to drown out the prisoners' words - rat tat tat tat. And when they couldn't – RAT TAT TAT TAT TAT.

Mary watched as Marmaduke Stephenson and William Robinson were hanged.

A man suddenly mounted the gallows. He had an announcement. The woman would not die today.

The hangman removed the noose, but Mary Dyer wouldn't step down. She had to be dragged from the gallows.

· · · · ᧼ᑯ · · · ·

Mary Dyer was born in England in 1611. Her family belonged to the Puritan religion. In the 1630s and 1640s, Puritans left England to escape religious **persecution.** Mary and her husband, William, moved to America in 1634.

TIDBITS

Not all Puritans felt the laws against Quakers were fair. They did not want to see Mary die. Many urged her to beg for pardon and return to Rhode Island. Mary refused.

••

The Puritans executed one more Quaker after Mary Dyer. His name was William Leddra. In all, four Quakers died in America in the name of religious freedom. Mary was the only woman.

The Puritans formed the Massachusetts Bay Colony. The leaders made laws about how people should worship. Surprisingly, Puritans persecuted people who went against *their* beliefs.

Mary and William began to follow the teachings of another Puritan, Anne Hutchinson. Anne was a strong, outspoken woman. She had different ideas about how to worship God.

Puritan leaders felt threatened by strong women. In 1638, they put Anne on trial where she was found guilty of **heresy**. Her sentence was announced in church. Anne would be **banished** from the Colony forever. In a bold show of support, Mary Dyer walked out of church with Anne.

The Puritans would be rid of Anne, but Mary presented a problem. They were afraid of what she would do next.

Governor John Winthrop wanted to stop Mary. He heard that she had given birth to a **stillborn**, **deformed** baby. Winthrop had the baby **exhumed**. He published a monstrous description of the child's body. Many believed the tale.

The Puritans said the baby was God's way of punishing Mary. The Dyers were forced from the Colony. They moved to Rhode Island. Here they worshiped as they wanted.

In 1652, the Dyers traveled to England. Mary learned about Quakers. Quakers believed people do not need ministers to help them worship. Mary became a Quaker. She returned to Boston in 1657. She was arrested and again banished.

In 1657, the Massachusetts Bay Colony passed terrible laws against Quakers. Their churches had to be kept secret. When found, Quakers were arrested and then banished. Some Quakers returned in **defiance** of the law. If they did, they risked having their ears cut off. They could also have their tongues bored through with a hot poker. If a Quaker returned again, the final punishment was death.

In 1659, Mary returned to Boston to challenge the laws. The Puritans arrested Mary. They sentenced her to be hanged with Stephenson and Robinson. Her husband begged for mercy. The governor of Connecticut asked that Mary be freed. Mary had to be dragged off the gallows. Seven months later, she returned to Boston knowing she risked death.

This time, the Puritans succeeded in silencing Mary. The General Court found her guilty of being a Quaker. On June 1, 1660, soldiers escorted Mary once more to Boston Common. She was hanged in front of a large crowd. Mary went to the gallows willingly. She believed her death would help change wicked Puritan laws.

The King of England heard the Puritans were hanging Quakers. He put a stop to it. Eventually, the colonists could worship freely.

Mary Dyer was willing to die for her religious beliefs.

TIDBITS

Almost 300 years after it sentenced her to death, the Massachusetts General Court had a statue of Mary Dyer erected at the State House in Boston. It was created by Quaker sculptor, Sylvia Shaw Judson.

•◆•

Mary is buried on Boston Common, but no one has been able to find her grave.

Timeline: Mary Dyer

1611	➤	Mary Barrett is born in England.
1633	➤	October 27, Mary and William Dyer wed in England.
1634	➤	The Dyers move to Massachusetts. Between 1634 and 1650, Mary gives birth to seven children who survive into adulthood.
1637	➤	October 17, Mary gives birth to dead, deformed baby girl.
1638	➤	March 22, Mary leaves the church with Anne Hutchinson. Mary is 27 years old.
		Governor John Winthrop has Mary's baby dug up.
		The Puritans ban the Dyers from Massachusetts.
1652	➤	Mary and William travel to England. Mary becomes a Quaker.
1656	➤	Massachusetts passes several laws against Quakers.
1657	➤	Mary returns from England. Mary is arrested. She is freed after her husband demands her release. He promises the Puritans that Mary will not return to Massachusetts.
		Mary travels the Rhode Island and New York countryside preaching Quakerism.
1658	➤	October 19, Massachusetts passes _by one vote_ a law banishing Quakers "upon pain of death."
1659	➤	June, Mary travels to Boston in support of her friends, Stephenson and Robinson, who were arrested for being Quakers. Mary is arrested and banished.
		September, Stephenson and Robinson are arrested again. Mary travels to Boston to support them. In October, the two men hang, but Mary is released.
1660	➤	Mary returns to Boston in **defiance** of the law. She does not tell her husband she's going. Mary is arrested and sentenced to death on May 31.
		June 1, Mary is hanged on Boston Common.
1959	➤	Massachusetts erects a bronze statue of Mary at the State House in Boston.

Learn More About Mary Dyer and Colonial Quakers

- Furbee, Mary Rodd. *Outrageous Women of Colonial America*. Jossey-Bass, 2001.

- Hinman, Bonnie. *The Massachusetts Bay Colony: The Puritans Arrive from England.* Mitchell Lane Publishers, 2006.

- Stille, Darlene R. *Anne Hutchinson: Puritan Protestor*. Compass Point Books, 2006.

- Yolen, Jane. *Friend: The Story of George Fox and the Quakers*. Houghton Miflin, 1972.

Websites:

- The history of Mary Dyer:
  http://www.rootsweb.ancestry.com/ ~ nwa/dyer.html
  http://www.mayflowerfamilies.com/enquirer/mary_dyer.htm

Glossary

banished (BAN isht) Sent away from a place and ordered not to return.

defiance (di FYE uhnss) The act of standing up to someone or to a group and refusing to obey.

deformed (di FORMD) Twisted, bent, or disfigured.

exhumed (ig ZOOMD) Taken out of the ground.

gallows (GAL ohz) A wooden frame used in the past for hanging criminals.

persecution (PUR suh kyoo shuhn) Treating someone cruelly and unfairly, especially because of the person's ideas or beliefs.

Quaker (KWAY kur) A member of the Society of Friends, a Christian group founded in 1650 that prefers simple religious services and opposes war.

stillborn (STIL born) A baby that is born dead.

— 2 —
Anne Dudley Bradstreet:
America's First Poet

by Kathleen W. Deady

*E*ighteen-year-old Anne clung to the railing of the *Arabella*. She stared into the early morning darkness. She had been 77 days on the open ocean. The ship was cramped and people were hungry. Many had died. Others were sick from illnesses such as **scurvy**.

Finally, they saw land. Yet Anne did not want to go ashore. There were no buildings or roads, no wheat fields or grazing sheep. There was only emptiness and unknown danger. Fear filled her. Would drowning at sea be better than facing what this strange New World offered?

· · · · ○ · · · ·

Anne Dudley was born in Northampton, England around 1612. She did not attend school, but was very well educated. Anne's father worked as the **steward** for the Earl of Lincoln. Her family lived on the **estate**. Anne used the Earl's library. She also had private tutors in literature, history, and languages.

Anne had a number of serious illnesses. As a young child, she was bedridden for a time with **rheumatic fever**. Later, Anne nearly died from **smallpox**. Periods of poor health would continue throughout her life.

At 16, Anne married Simon Bradstreet. Simon was 25 and worked for Anne's father on the Earl's estate. The Dudleys and the Bradstreets were **Puritans.** The Puritans were unhappy with the Church of England. They wanted to **worship** in their own way. In 1630, the Bradstreets and others left England for the New World.

Anne did not want to leave her home. She knew life in America would be difficult. But Anne hid her fears. Instead she accepted this change as what God wanted for her.

It took three months for the Puritans to sail to Salem Harbor. Conditions in the tiny settlement were poor. The settlers there were sick and dying. They had few supplies. Anne's father soon moved the family to nearby Charlestown for the winter. Later, they moved several more times to improve their conditions and increase their land.

Anne began writing poems about her life. In 1632, after another extended illness, she wrote "Upon a Fit of Sickness." This is the earliest poem of Anne's that we know exists. Soon after she recovered, Anne and Simon had their first child.

Slowly, life got better as the colony grew. Simon became a leader. He often was called away. Anne raised their growing family and ran the household. She also wrote many poems.

In 1647, Anne's brother-in-law traveled to England. He

TIDBITS

Twelve ships sailed to the New World. They carried around 1000 Puritans. The *Arabella* was the lead ship. This began what would be called the Great Migration (1630-1642).

•◆•

The first winter in the new colony would later be called "the starvation time."

•◆•

Anne's first book of poems was called *The Tenth Muse Lately Sprung Up in America*. It was the only work of Anne's published in her lifetime.

TIDBITS

Anne lost a collection of over 800 books when their house burned. After the fire, she wrote her poem "*Upon the Burning of Our House July 10, 1666.*"

•—•—•

It is uncertain whether Anne is buried next to her husband in "the old Burying Point" in Salem, or in "the Old Burying Ground" on Academy Road in North Andover.

brought copies of Anne's poems to show a publisher. It is believed he did this without her knowledge or permission. Anne's first book of poems was published there in 1650.

Anne was surprised and embarrassed by the book's success. She felt the poems were not polished. She later revised many of them. A second edition was published after she died.

Anne's family life was very busy. In 1666, tragedy struck. Her house burned to the ground. The Bradstreets lost all of their belongings, including some of Anne's unpublished work.

Anne continued to write of her life, including the deaths of several grandchildren. Much of her later work is more personal. It is considered much stronger than her earlier work.

However, once again her health declined. In 1672, Anne's daughter Dorothy died. Deeply saddened by her losses and weakened by illness, Anne died a few months later.

Anne was America's first poet. Her poems reveal a woman of great strength and character. They tell a lot about a woman's life during America's early years.

To My Dear and Loving Husband

If ever two were one, then surely we.

If ever man were lov'd by wife, then thee;

If ever wife was happy in a man,

Compare with me, ye women, if you can.

Anne's most famous poem "*To My Dear and Loving Husband*" is still very popular today. People often recite the poem at weddings.

Timeline: Anne Dudley Bradstreet

c1612 ➤ Anne is born in Northampton, England to Thomas Dudley and Dorothy Yorke Dudley, the second of five children.

c1619 ➤ Her father takes a job as steward to the Earl of Lincoln. The family moves to Earl's household in Sempringham in Lincolnshire.

1628 ➤ At 16 years old, Anne marries Simon Bradstreet.

1630 ➤ March 29, Anne, Simon, and their families leave England on the *Arabella* and sail to the Massachusetts Bay Colony in America.

June 12, arrive at Salem Harbor, soon move to Charlestown, where they spend the winter.

1631 ➤ Moves in the spring to Newtown, now Cambridge.

1632 ➤ Has lingering illness, which she would later describe "like a consumption" or what we call **tuberculosis**. Composes first known poem, *Upon a Fit of Sickness.*

1633 ➤ Gives birth to first child, Samuel.

1635–1652 ➤ Has seven more children, Dorothy (1635), Sarah (1638), Simon (1640), Hanna (1642), Mercy (1645), Dudley (1648), and John (1652).

1635 ➤ Moves with first two children, Samuel and Dorothy, to Agawam, now Ipswich.

1645 ➤ Moves again to help settle Andover, with their first five children. Sixth child, Mercy born a few months later.

1647 ➤ Brother-in-law travels to England, taking with him Anne's poems to submit to a publisher.

1650 ➤ Publishes her first book of poems, *The Tenth Muse Lately Sprung Up in America.*

1672 ➤ February 26, daughter Dorothy dies, the only one of Anne's children to die before her.

September 16, Anne dies in Andover at the age of 60, it is believed of tuberculosis.

1678 ➤ Revised edition of *The Tenth Muse* is published.

NOTE: c1612 means about or around 1612

Learn More about Anne Bradstreet, Puritans, and the Massachusetts Bay Colony

- Deady, Kathleen W. *The Massachusetts Bay Colony*. Capstone Press, 2006.
- Hinman, Bonnie. *The Massachusetts Bay Colony: The Puritans Arrive from England*. Mitchell Lane Publishers, 2006.

Websites:

- Biography of Anne Bradstreet:
  http://www.annebradstreet.com
- Essay written in Memory of Anne Bradstreet:
  http://www.massmoments.org/moment.cfm?mid = 265

Glossary

estate (ess TATE) A large area of land, usually with a house on it.

Puritans (PYOOR uh tuhnz) One of a group of English Protestants in the 16th and 17th centuries who believed in a strict code of behavior and who believed worship should be simple, without music and ceremony.

rheumatic fever (roo MA tik FEE vuhr) A serious disease that causes fever, joint pain, and possible heart damage.

scurvy (SKUR vee) A disease caused by a lack of Vitamin C in the diet. Those suffering from the disease often have great weakness and bleeding gums.

steward (STOO urd) A person who serves food and drink to a wealthy land owner.

tuberculosis (tu BUR kyuh LOH siss) A highly contagious bacterial disease that usually affects the lungs.

worship (WUR ship) To express love and devotion to God or to a god.

— 3 —

Rebecca Towne Nurse:
The Salem Witch Trials

by Andrea Murphy

Rebecca had been sick nearly a week. Someone was knocking on the door. She struggled to rise from her chair. Her old bones ached with every movement, but she had to greet the guests.

They talked of Betty Parris, one of the village girls who had been **bewitched**. It was all anybody spoke of that winter in 1692.

"I **grieve** for Mr. Parris and his family," Rebecca said. "But I fear some spoken of as witches are innocent."

"Rebecca," said one visitor. "You are spoken of as a witch also."

Rebecca sat stunned. When she found her voice, she said, "As to this thing I am as innocent as the child unborn . . ."

· · · · ৩৩ · · · ·

Rebecca Towne was born in Great Yarmouth, England around 1621. Rebecca's parents were **Puritans.** They were unhappy with the Church of England. By 1640, the Townes left England for America.

TIDBITS

Nurse is often seen spelled as "Nourse" in many documents.

• ◆ •

Colonial people believed in evil witches. They thought these witches went after children. This made it easy for people to believe that witches lived among them.

• ◆ •

Rebecca's mother was said to be a witch. Two of Rebecca's sisters, Mary Towne Easty and Sarah Towne Cloyce, also were accused of witchcraft. Mary was hanged on September 22, 1692.

The Towne family settled in Topsfield, Massachusetts. Around 1644, Rebecca married Francis Nurse. They moved to Salem, Massachusetts. Francis worked as a tray maker. Rebecca kept house, and raised her growing family. She would have four daughters and four sons.

Colonial New England was a harsh place. Much of the land was wilderness. Winters were long and cold. Everybody, even the children, worked.

Rebecca was known as a good and religious woman. She taught her children the Puritan ways. They rarely played, and they never complained. They did not show their emotions. They learned about the Bible.

In February 1692, the minister's daughter fell ill. Ten-year old Betty Parris's body jerked. She screamed as if in great pain. She ran wildly around the room. She crawled under furniture. Some people suspected witchcraft.

Other girls began having fits. Their bodies twisted. They fell to the floor and lay frozen. They said that **specters** bit and pinched them. The village doctor could find no cure. He said the cause might be **supernatural**.

Eleven-year old Ann Putnam was caught in the **hysteria**. She claimed to see witches flying through the air. She said a specter bit and pinched her. Ann did not know the specter's name, but knew where she sat at the meeting house. Rebecca's name was suggested to her. Only then did Ann name old Rebecca Nurse as the witch who tormented her.

Soon, others insisted Rebecca had hurt them. Rebecca was pulled from her sick bed and arrested. Many in the community could not believe it. To support Rebecca, thirty-nine people signed a **petition**. It said Rebecca could not have done these things.

On March 24, 1692, Rebecca faced those who accused her in court. The girls became hysterical at the sight of Rebecca.

The judge said, "**Goody** Nurse. Here are two. Ann Putman the child and Abigail Williams complains of your hurting them. What do you say to it?"

"I can say before my Eternal Father I am innocent and God will clear my innocency," Rebecca said.

Rebecca did not get a fair trial. The judges acted like she was guilty. Even so, the jury found Rebecca not guilty on June 30, 1692.

Her accusers screamed and fell to the floor. The judges told the jury to try again. This time, the jury declared Rebecca guilty.

On July 19, 1692, Rebecca was hanged at Gallows Hill in Salem.

Innocent people were accused of witchcraft.

TIDBITS

The Townes and the Putnams argued over land for years. It is possible that young Ann Putnam knew about the bad feelings between the families. Perhaps this made it easy for Ann to accuse Rebecca Towne Nurse as a witch.

Rebecca's body was buried near Gallows Hill. Her children secretly removed her body the night she was executed. They brought it back to Rebecca's beloved homestead, and buried it in an unmarked grave.

Timeline: Rebecca Towne Nurse

c1621 ➤ Rebecca is born the first of eight children to William and Joanna Towne in Great Yarmouth, England. She is baptized on February 21, 1621.

c1640 ➤ The Townes immigrate to America.

c1644 ➤ Rebecca marries Francis Nurse. They will have eight children.

1692 ➤ Around March 14, Rebecca is named as a witch by Ann Putnam Jr. [sic]

March 23, Rebecca is arrested.

June 30, the jury finds Rebecca not guilty. The judges tell the jury to reconsider. The jury finds Rebecca guilty. She is sentenced to death.

July 3, Rebecca is **excommunicated** from her church.

July 19, Rebecca is hanged for witchcraft on Gallows Hill in Salem, Massachusetts.

1706 ➤ Ann Putnam Jr. publicly apologizes for her part in the Salem witch hunt.

1885 ➤ The Nurse family erects a memorial to Rebecca.

1908 ➤ The homestead is purchased and restored by the Rebecca Nurse Memorial Association.

1926 ➤ The property is given to the Society for the Preservation of New England Antiquities.

1981 ➤ The Danvers Alarm List Company Incorporated, assumes ownership of the homestead.

NOTE: c1621 means about or around 1621

Learn More about Rebecca Nurse and the Salem Witch Trials

- Dunn, Joeming. *The Salem Witch Trials (Graphic History Set 2)*. Graphic Planet, 2008.

- Nardo, Don. *The Salem Witch Trials (American History)*. Lucent Books, 2007.

- Magoon, Kekla. *The Salem Witch Trials (Essential Events)*. Abdo Publishing Company, 2008.

- Price, Sean. *Salem Witch Trials: Colonial Life (History Through Primary Sources)*. Raintree, 2008.

Websites:

- The Rebecca Nurse Homestead and the Salem Witch Trials: http://www.rebeccanurse.org/RNurse/Homestead.htm

- A website about the Salem Witch Trials: http://www.law.umkc.edu/faculty/projects/ftrials/salem/SAL_BNUR.HTM

- How did it feel to be accused of witchcraft? http://www.nationalgeographic.com/salem/

Glossary

bewitched (bi WICHT) Having a magic spell cast on.

excommunicated (eks kuh MYOO nuh kate id) Cut off officially from a church.

Goody (GUD ee) Short form of Goodwife. A married woman of low social status.

grieve (GREEV) To feel great sadness, usually over the death of a loved one.

hysteria (hi STER ee uh) An uncontrolled emotional outburst usually caused by fear.

meeting house (MEE ting HOUSS) A building where church services are held.

petition (puh TISH uhn) A letter signed by many people requesting a change in policy.

Puritans (PYOOR uh tuhnz) One of a group of English Protestants in the 16th and 17th centuries who believed in a strict code of behavior and who believed worship should be simple, without music and ceremony.

specters (SPEK turz) Ghosts.

supernatural (SOO pur NACH ur uhl) Involving things that the laws of nature cannot explain.

— 4 —
Abigail Adams:
First Lady of the United States

by M. Lu Major

June 17, 1775

Abigail Adams brought her eight-year-old son, John Quincy, to the top of Boston's Penn's Hill. They watched British soldiers attacking American volunteers. The fighting in the fields below was loud and bloody. But Abigail wanted her son to understand the importance of this war.

Later, Abigail wrote to her husband, John, about the battle. "The Day…is come on which the fate of America depends." The American colonies wanted freedom from England. Now, Abigail believed, independence seemed possible.

What Abigail did not know yet, was that she was writing to a future president of the new country. And the little boy who stood by her on Penn's Hill? He, one day, would lead the United States, too.

· · · · ◎ · · · ·

Abigail Smith was born on November 11, 1744 in Weymouth, Massachusetts. Her father was a minister. Her mother was a homemaker.

22

In the 1700s, few girls attended school. Abigail's mother taught her to read and write. She learned some math. The rest of Abigail's education came from her father's library.

Around 1759, Abigail met John Adams, a lawyer. They married five years later. At that time, women were thought to be less intelligent than men. John Adams, however, believed in his wife's abilities. The couple discussed everything. They talked about the running of their farm. They discussed their family. And they talked about politics.

When Great Britain and America went to war, some men fought for freedom. Others, like John Adams, prepared for a new government. John spent months in Philadelphia at the **Continental Congress**. Abigail was left alone to care for their children, home, and farm. She knew America's women would have to make sacrifices for freedom, too.

Abigail wrote to John nearly every day. She encouraged him: "Your task is difficult and important." Abigail understood that the delegates were writing new laws. She asked John "… [that] you would Remember the Ladies…" Abigail hoped the delegates would create a government that would give women more rights.

During the war, John went to France to ask for soldiers and supplies. Abigail knew this separation would be long. Sea voyages took months. John was gone for two years. Then, only months after he returned, he left for England to **negotiate** a peace treaty.

In those days, a man forced away from his home and

TIDBITS

It was not unusual for people to gather to watch battles. Nearly 100 years later, people took picnics to watch the first major battle of the Civil War near Manassas, Virginia.

◆ ◆

Abigail Adams was the first woman to become both the wife and the mother of a United States President. She did not live to see her son, John Quincy Adams, become the sixth President of the United States in 1825.

TIDBITS

Abigail Adams was the first First Lady to live in the White House. She only lived there a total of four months. The building was not yet complete. Abigail hung her wet laundry in the unfinished East Room.

◆—◆

Forty years after Abigail's death, some of her letters were organized into a book and published by her grandson. It was the first time a book about a First Lady had been compiled.

business would have asked another man to run things. John put his faith in Abigail. She raised their children. She hired farmhands. She kept the family from **bankruptcy** during war time. Abigail rented out some of their property. She went after people who owed John money for legal work. She sold goods John sent from Europe.

After the war, John became the first Vice President of the United States. At first, Philadelphia was America's capital. Abigail had new duties to perform. When she could, she left Massachusetts and went to Philadelphia to help John. She entertained visitors nearly every night. To save money, she prepared most of the meals herself.

Abigail was John's trusted **confidante** when he became the country's second president. Even John's advisors missed Abigail when she was away from the president. "Oh, how they **lament** Mrs. Adam's absence! She is a good counselor!" John wrote to her.

Finally, after 36 years of marriage, Abigail had her husband home. His presidency over, John returned to their farm. For twelve years they lived a quiet, happy life.

When Abigail was 73, she became ill with **typhus**. She died on October 28, 1818.

The "Old House" in Quincy, Massachusetts was home to John & Abigail Adams.

Timeline: Abigail Adams

1744	➤	November 11, born in Weymouth, Massachusetts to Reverend William and Elizabeth Quincy Smith. She is their second child.
1752	➤	Calendar revised. Abigail's birthday celebration changes to November 22.
1764	➤	October 25, marries lawyer, John Adams.
1765–1772	➤	Gives birth to children, Abigail (Nabby) (1765), John Quincy (1767), Susanna (1768), Charles (1770), and Thomas (1772).
1774	➤	Gives birth to a still-born daughter, Elizabeth.
		John Adams serves as the Massachusetts Colony's delegate to the First Continental Congress. Abigail begins writing letters to him that will become important historical documents.
1775	➤	Abigail is elected by the Massachusetts Colony General Court (along with two other women) to question other wives about their loyalty to the American cause.
1776	➤	Abigail's letters to John during the Second Continental Congress become some of the earliest known writings that call for equal rights for women.
1777	➤	June, gives birth to a stillborn daughter.
		Abigail spends the next two years alone as John leaves to represent the American colonies in France. He brings their son, John Quincy, with him.
1779	➤	June, John returns home from France.
		November, the Continental Congress sends John to England to negotiate peace. Abigail protects the family's finances during the war.
1784	➤	Abigail, daughter Nabby, and son John Quincy join John Adams in Europe.
1787	➤	Abigail and John buy a large farm which they name "Peacefield."
1789	➤	John Adams becomes the first Vice President of the United States. Abigail spends part of each year with him as the nation's capital moves from New York to Philadelphia.
1797	➤	John Adams becomes President of the United States. Abigail does not attend his inauguration because she is caring for John's dying mother.
1818	➤	October 28, Abigail dies at home in Quincy, Massachusetts.

Learn More About Abigail Adams, and the American Revolution

- Dubois, Muriel L. *John Adams (Photo Illustrated Biographies).* Bridgestone Books, 2003.

- Lakin, Patricia. *Abigail Adams: First Lady of the American Revolution.* Fitzgerald Books, 2007.

- Mayer, Cassie. *Abigail Adams (First Biographies).* Heinneman, 2007.

- Whiting, Jim. *Abigail Adams (Profiles in American History).* Mitchell Lane Publishers, 2008.

Websites:

- A White House biography:
  http://www.whitehouse.gov/history/firstladies/aa2.html

- The National First Ladies Library:
  http://www.firstladies.org/biographies/firstladies.aspx?biography = 2

Glossary

bankruptcy (BANGK ruhpt see) Having no money. Being unable to pay one's debts.

confidante (KON fi dawnt) A person to whom one can tell secrets.

Continental Congress (KON tuh NENT uhl KONG ress) During the American Revolution, the governing body of the thirteen original colonies that would become the United States.

lament (luh MENT) To show great sadness or disappointment.

negotiate (ni GOH shee ate) To bargain; to discuss something so as to reach an agreement.

typhus (TYE fuss) A serious disease marked by a red rash and high fever. The disease was often spread by lice.

— 5 —
Elizabeth Porter Phelps:
Diary-Keeper

by Sally Wilkins

Elizabeth took the last pie from the oven in front of the fireplace and placed it on the table. She stood back and counted. Eight pumpkin, ten apple, five cranberry. She hoped it would be enough. With grandchildren now, Thanksgiving was an even bigger gathering. Tomorrow they would make a dozen chicken pies.

She pulled a goose **quill** from the jar of sand on the hearth and examined the tip. Dare she steal half an hour? She could record the day's accomplishments in her diary or add to the letter she was writing to her cousin. But making a pen would take time. She would need a candle at her desk. Four o'clock would come quickly, she knew. The pleasure of the pen would have to wait for another day.

· · · · ৩ · · · ·

Elizabeth Porter was born in Hadley, Massachusetts in 1747. An only child, she loved to write. Her journals and letters left a wonderful record of daily life in early America.

TIDBITS

Both Elizabeth's parents came from wealthy farm families known as the River Gods, the **elite** class in the Connecticut Valley villages. The River Gods were not pleased when Elizabeth chose to marry Charles Phelps instead of the man her uncles had chosen for her.

◆•◆

Elizabeth made her wedding gown from French silk, because the Colonists were **boycotting** English imports.

In 1752 her father, Moses Porter moved his family out of the village to a new farm he called Forty Acres. Two years later, he went to fight in the **French and Indian War**. Moses died when his company was **ambushed.**

Elizabeth and her mother stayed at Forty Acres. Elizabeth learned to manage the tasks of both the house and the farm. She cared for her mother, who suffered from **depression**. Elizabeth's journals record hard work. She carried water and scrubbed floors. She helped slaughter hogs and pluck chickens. There were fun times, too. Elizabeth's letters to her cousin Penelope tell of sleighing parties, picnics and singing school.

Elizabeth married Charles Phelps in 1770. They had three children. One baby died. A son and a daughter grew up. Elizabeth also raised a baby girl whose mother had died.

Over the next forty years the Phelpses expanded and improved the farm. They raised all their vegetables, fruit and meat. They made candles and soap from the fat of their animals. They sold what they did not use. Elizabeth was known for her cheese making. At night she stitched the household's clothing by hand, sewing late into the evening.

Success brought responsibility. Forty Acres often provided shelter to travelers. During the Revolution Charles and Elizabeth housed British prisoners of war. Elizabeth took in unwed mothers and families in trouble. Elizabeth was often called to come to people's houses when women were ill or giving birth. She kept a basket of medicinal herbs for these visits.

A large farm required many workers. The Phelpses kept a few black slaves and white **indentured servants**. They hired people from the village to work during busy times. Servants, slaves, hired help, and travelers all ate with the family. Elizabeth often made dinner for twenty to thirty people. Her diary reports many days of getting up at 3 am and working until after dark. No wonder she enjoyed the quiet **Sabbath** afternoons when she sharpened her quills and recorded her thoughts.

Elizabeth died in 1817, one year after her daughter Betsey had moved back to the farm. With Betsey's eleven children, Elizabeth's home housed a busy family once again.

A photograph of Elizabeth Phelps' glasses and diary.

TIDBITS

After the Revolution (in 1782) a **Hessian** soldier, Andries, and his wife Mary came to live and work at Forty Acres. They introduced the celebration of Christmas.

For many years children sleeping at Forty Acres reported waking up to see Elizabeth's ghost tucking them into bed.

In 1949 James Lincoln Huntington, Elizabeth's great-great-grandson, turned Forty Acres into a museum.

29

Timeline: Elizabeth Porter Phelps

1747 ➤ November 24, Elizabeth Porter is born in Hadley, Massachusetts, the only child of Moses Porter and Elizabeth Pitkin.

1752 ➤ Moses Porter builds a showcase house and farm two miles outside the village.

1755 ➤ Moses leads the Hadley militia to New York to battle the French. He dies in an ambush.

1763 ➤ Elizabeth begins keeping a diary. She records sermon texts, village events, and later, daily accomplishments.

1770 ➤ Elizabeth marries Charles Phelps.

1772 ➤ August, Elizabeth's first child is born, Moses Porter Phelps.

1776 ➤ December, Elizabeth's second son, Charles, is born. He lives just one week. Soon after, Elizabeth takes in a two-week-old baby girl, Thankful Richmond, whose mother has died.

1777 ➤ March, Charles and Elizabeth take in prisoners captured from the British ship at Boston. One, a Scot name John Morison, becomes the Phelps' gardener. He remains on the farm until his death in 1814.

1779 ➤ February, Elizabeth (Betsey) Whiting Phelps is born.

1787 ➤ January, the Phelps farm provides food for the militia fighting rebels in Western Massachusetts (Shay's Rebellion).

1791 ➤ December, Elizabeth takes in Susannah Whipple and her six-week-old daughter Submit. "Mitte" would stay on with Elizabeth when Susannah marries three years later.

1798 ➤ January 28, Charles Phelps Hitchcock, Elizabeth's first grandchild, is born at Forty Acres.

1798 ➤ September, Elizabeth's mother dies.

1814 ➤ Charles Phelps dies.

1816 ➤ Elizabeth's daughter Betsey, with her husband Daniel Huntington and their eleven children, returns to the family home.

1817 ➤ Elizabeth Porter Phelps dies.

Learn More about Elizabeth Porter Phelps and Colonial America

- Bjornlund, Lydia D. *Women in Colonial America.* Gale Group, 2003.
- Day, Nancy. *Your Travel Guide to Colonial America.* Runestone Press, 2001.
- Johnson, Claudia Durst *Daily Life in Colonial New England.* Greenwood Press, 2002.
- Erickson, Stephen C. "The Porter-Phelps-Huntington House," New England Genealogical Society. December, 1987.

Websites:

- Official website of Porter-Phelps-Huntington House museum: www.pphmuseum.org
- Deerfield Massachusetts was a community similar to Hadley: www.deerfield-ma.org/

Glossary

ambushed (AM busht) Attacked by someone who was hidden from sight.

boycotting (BOI kot ing) Refusing to buy something as a way of protesting.

depression (di PRESH uhn) A mental illness in which a person suffers from deep sadness.

elite (i LEET) A group of people who have special advantages or privileges.

French and Indian War (FRENCH and IN dee uhn WOR) A series of battles between Great Britain and the American colonists against the French and their Native American allies. The war lasted from 1754 to 1763.

Hessian (HESH uhn) German soldiers sent to help the British during the American Revolution.

indentured servant (in DEN chuhrd SUR vuhnt) A person who worked for 5 to 7 years without pay in exchange for payment of the person's passage to the American colonies.

medicinal herb (me DI suh Nuhl URB) A plant used specifically for treating illness.

quill (KWIL) A pen made from a bird's feather. The tip of the feather was carved to form a point.

Sabbath (SAB uhth) The day of rest and worship in some religions.

selectman (suh LEKT muhn) One of the people elected to run town affairs.

— 6 —

Lucretia Coffin Mott:
Suffragette and Abolitionist

by Janet Buell

*L*ucretia's mother held the newborn girl in her arms. Anna Coffin hoped the best for her tiny daughter. She didn't know then that Lucretia would grow up to shake America to its very core.

· · · · ∽ · · · ·

Lucretia Mott was born in 1793. America was a much different place than it is now. Women could not vote. They were bound to the laws men made for them. A woman's property became her husband's when they married. In divorce, the man had all rights to the couple's children. Women could not go to college. They could not hold jobs usually held by men. A woman could not be elected to office. It was a time when Americans could own other people as property.

Lucretia's parents were Quakers. Quakers had different ideas about men and women. Thomas and Anna Coffin believed in equality for both.

They sent Lucretia and her sister to a Quaker **boarding school** in New York. Here Lucretia met James Mott. They married in 1811. James would prove to be a loving and supportive husband.

In 1817, Lucretia spoke powerfully at Quaker meeting. She spoke out against slavery. The Quakers were impressed by what Lucretia had to say. They made her a Quaker minister. Lucretia traveled throughout New England preaching her anti-slavery views.

Lucretia and James became delegates to the World Anti-Slavery Convention. The men decided to block women's attendance at the meeting. Lucretia and the other women had to sit behind a screen. They could not speak their views.

Lucretia met Elizabeth Cady Stanton at the convention. Elizabeth was the wife of a delegate. Lucretia and Elizabeth talked about America's unfair laws. They knew women's votes and women's voices could help make slavery illegal. The two women began a lifelong friendship.

Lucretia, Elizabeth, and two other women organized the first Woman's Rights convention. The women revised the Declaration of Independence. Their Declaration of **Sentiments** asked men to grant women rights equal to theirs.

Only a handful of women had ever spoken out against the **status quo**. Many women now spoke out. News of the convention sparked outrage among men *and* women. Women were meant to be housewives, they said. Men were meant to run businesses, cities, states, and the country.

TIDBITS

Lucretia became one of the founders of the Philadelphia Female Anti-Slavery Society. Lucretia also helped organize the first Anti-Slavery Convention of American Women.

◆━◆

People sought out Lucretia for her powerful **oratory**. She traveled all over the country speaking to mixed groups of men and women about abolition. Some were shocked by this behavior. They considered it unladylike for a woman to speak to anyone but groups of women.

TIDBITS

Lucretia loved to raise children and keep house. She also liked being hostess to the many people who visited her home.

◆•◆

Lucretia and James practiced what they preached. James was a cloth merchant who refused to sell cotton cloth because it was made by slaves.

The outrage against these **"uppity"** women continued for many years. Much of the criticism fell on Lucretia. Newspapers printed **editorials** condemning her actions. Lucretia tried her best to ignore the comments. She carried on, but suffered severe stomach pains. The pains were likely brought on by stress.

This pain didn't stop Lucretia. She continued to work throughout her life for human rights. The Civil War eventually freed the slaves. Men finally gave women the right to vote in 1920. Lucretia had been dead for forty years by that time.

Lucretia Mott spent a lifetime talking to Americans. She tried to convince them to think differently about blacks and women. She worked tirelessly to free the slaves. She raised money to help poor people. She and James raised money for the first medical school for women. Lucretia participated in several Peace Societies. The woman from Nantucket had become a leader for **abolition** and women's rights.

Several thousand people came to the cemetery to bid her good-bye when she died. They came to honor the tiny, outspoken woman. Lucretia had grown up to shake America to its core.

Let woman then go on, not asking favors, but claiming as right, the removal of all hindrances to her elevation in the scale of being.
—LUCRETIA MOTT.

A portrait of Lucretia Mott from the scrapbook kept by suffragettes Elizabeth and Anne Miller.

Timeline: Lucretia Coffin Mott

1793 ➤ January 3, Lucretia is born on Nantucket to Thomas and Anna Folger Coffin.

1806 ➤ Enters Nine Partners Quaker School in Dutchess County, New York.

1811 ➤ April 10, marries James Mott.

1812–1828 ➤ Lucretia gives birth to six children, five of whom survive into adulthood.

1830 ➤ Is elected clerk of the Philadelphia Yearly Women's Meeting. She holds the position for five years.

1833 ➤ Helps organize the Philadelphia Female Anti-Slavery Society.

1837 ➤ Attends the first Anti-Slavery Convention of American Women, which she helps organize.

1840 ➤ Lucretia and James attend the World's Anti-Slavery Convention held in London.

1848 ➤ May 9, Lucretia makes her first major speech at the American Anti-Slavery Society in New York.

July 13, meets with Elizabeth Cady Stanton and three other women. The five women hatch a plan for the first national woman's rights convention.

July 19–20, attends the Seneca Falls convention.

1850 ➤ Attends First National Woman's Rights Convention in Worcester, MA.

1851 ➤ The passage of the **Fugitive Slave Act** in 1850 prompts Lucretia and James to work even harder for abolition.

1852 ➤ Elected President of Woman's Rights convention in Syracuse, New York.

1864 ➤ April 1, draws up charter that starts Swarthmore College. The college is the first to admit both men and women.

1866 ➤ May, chosen as first president of the Equal Rights Association meeting in New York.

1868 ➤ James dies.

1876 ➤ Presides over the National Woman Suffrage Association meeting in Philadelphia.

1878 ➤ July 19, delivers her last public speech at Rochester, New York on the 30th anniversary of the Seneca Falls convention.

1880 ➤ November 11, Lucretia dies at Roadside, her farm near Philadelphia.

Learn More About Lucretia Mott and the Fight for Equal Rights

- Davis, Lucile. *Lucretia Mott: A Photo-Illustrated Biography.* Bridgestone Books, 1998.

- De Angelis, Gina. *Lucretia Mott*. Chelsea House Publishers, 2001.

- Tackach, James. *The Abolition of American Slavery (World History Series).* Lucent Books, 2002.

Websites:

- Living the Legacy: the Women's Rights Movement 1848-1998: http://www.legacy98.org/move-hist.html

Glossary

abolished (uh BOL ishd) Put an end to something officially. *The 13th Amendment to the U.S. Constitution abolished slavery.*

convention (kuhn VEN shuhn) A large gathering of people who have the same interests, such as a political meeting to choose candidates for election.

delegates (DEL uh guhtss) People who represent others at meetings.

editorials (ED uh TOR ee uhlz) Articles that reflect the opinions of a newspaper or magazine editor.

Fugitive Slave Act (FYOO juh tiv SLAYV akt) A law passed in 1850 that allowed federal agents to capture runaway slaves and return them to their owners.

oratory (OR uh tor ee) The art of speaking in public.

sentiments (SEN tuh muhntss) Opinions about specific matters; thoughts or attitudes based on feelings instead of reasoning.

status quo (STAT uhss kwoh) A Latin phrase meaning the state of affairs at this moment in time.

uppity (UH puh tee) Arrogant; conceited; too proud.

Dorothea Lynde Dix: Friend of the Friendless

by Sally Wilkins

*D*orothea visited the women prisoners after Sunday School class. A distant howl interrupted them. She looked at the guard. "What was that?"

"Nothing, Miss," he said. "One of the crazy ones."

Dorothea listened. Again the frightful scream. "Take me there."

The guard reluctantly unbarred a thick door. The air was frigid. It stank of human waste. Inside a bare stone room Dorothea saw two cages. An older woman covered with just a few rags ranted in one. In the other one a young woman knelt on the floor, covering her ears.

Dorothea Dix had stumbled upon her life's work.

· · · · ૭૦ · · · ·

Dorothea Dix was born in Hampden, Maine in 1802. Her father Joseph was a traveling preacher. He was often away for weeks at a time. Her mother Mary spent many of those days in bed, with no energy for her three children. Little Dorothea cooked and cleaned.

Dorothea's grandfather was a successful Boston doctor. Dorothea loved visiting her grandparents. There she could read and study. When she was twelve Dorothea ran away to her grandmother's. Her grandmother sent her to live with an aunt in Worcester. Two years later Dorothy began teaching. She put her hair up and wore long skirts to look older.

For twenty years Dorothea taught school, worked as a **governess**, and wrote books. After her father died she sent money to her mother and brothers.

Fits of coughing and high fever forced Dorothea to bed for weeks at a time. In 1836 she planned a trip to Italy to recover. The ocean crossing nearly killed her. Friends took her off the boat in England. They nursed her nearly a year before she was strong enough to walk downstairs. She stayed in England several months more, visiting hospitals and prisons with her friends.

While she was in England, Dorothea's grandmother died. Dorothea returned to Boston a wealthy woman. She volunteered to teach a Sunday School class for women in the Cambridge prison. There she discovered the cages.

In the 1800s most people were afraid of **mental illness.** Many thought **insane** people could not feel cold or pain. Wealthy families kept insane relatives locked up at home. Other insane people were put in prison.

Dorothea remembered visiting pleasant hospitals for the insane in England. She believed **humane** treatment could cure most mental disorders. She knew pain and hunger would make them worse. She believed even people who could not be cured should be treated as God's children.

Dorothea traveled across Massachusetts, taking careful notes. She found men, women, and children chained in dungeons or shut in crates. They were fed animal feed and garbage. Most wore rags or nothing at all.

After each journey, Dorothea wrote detailed descriptions from her notes. She convinced important men to present her reports to the **legislature**. She asked lawmakers to vote to build mental hospitals. Many opposed raising taxes to care for the insane. Dorothea worked hard to convince them.

For forty years, Dorothea criss-crossed the United States, Canada and Europe. Her friends were amazed. The woman who had been unable to get out of bed now rode for days in wagons, steamboats, and trains. She trekked through the wilderness and crawled into dungeons. Then she talked the powerful into caring for the powerless.

In 1881, Dorothea was ready to retire. She was old and tired and sick. But she had no home! The very first hospital she had designed offered her a room. She died there in 1887.

An illustration in the Capitol Building in Washington, D.C. shows Dorothea treating wounded Civil War soldiers.

TIDBITS

From 1842 to 1845, Dorothea traveled more than 10,000 miles.

◆

Sarah Josepha Hale wanted to include Dorothea in her book *Lives and Characters of Distinguished Women*, but Dorothea refused.

◆

Despite her work in legislation, Dorothea never affiliated with the suffragettes, fearing that those opposed to votes for women would also oppose her work for the insane.

Timeline: Dorothea Lynde Dix

1802	➤	April 4, Dorothea Lynde Dix born in Hampden, Maine oldest child of Joseph and Mary Dix.
1809	➤	Beloved grandfather, Dr. Elijah Dix, dies.
1814	➤	Leaves a note for her father and runs away. Grandmother sends her to live with an aunt in Worcester.
1816	➤	While living in Worcester, teaches children of family friends. Meets fiancé Edward Bangs.
1821	➤	Joseph Dix dies. Dorothea and brother Charles move to Boston. Dorothea attends William Ellery Channing's Unitarian church.
1824	➤	First book published, a "question and answer" book for children called *Conversations on Common Things*. It provided her with a steady income for forty years.
1826	➤	Illness forces her to give up teaching. Becomes a governess for the Channing children.
1836	➤	Sent to Italy to recuperate from illness, instead spends fourteen months in England.
1837	➤	Mother and Grandmother die, Dorothea returns to Boston.
1838	➤	Challenges court to provide heat for insane women in East Cambridge prison.
1839–1853	➤	Travels through United States and Canada documenting conditions of mental health patients.
1854–1881	➤	Travels and campaigns for hospitals for mentally ill throughout United States.
1861–1867	➤	Organizes Army nurse volunteers, insisting that Union and Confederate wounded be treated equally. Works in Union hospitals until the last patients were discharged in September 1867.
1881	➤	Too sick to travel, Dorothea retires to a room at the New Jersey State Lunatic Asylum in Trenton.
1887	➤	July 17, Dorothea dies in New Jersey. She is buried in Mt. Auburn Cemetery, Cambridge, MA.

Learn More About Dorothea Lynde Dix

- Muckenhoupt, Margaret. *Dorothea Dix: Advocate for Mental Health Care.* Oxford University Press, 2003.

- Witteman, Barbara. *Dorothea Dix: Social Reformer.* Bridgestone Books, 2003.

Websites:

- A biographical sketch of Dorothea Dix from the North Carolina hospital named for her:
  http://www.ncdhhs.gov/mhddsas/DIX/dorothea.html

- Very short piece from the Smithsonian Massachusetts Foundation for the Humanities:
  http://www.civilwar.si.edu/leaders_dix.html

- The Massachusetts State House Women's Leadership Project:
  http://www.mfh.org/specialprojects/shwlp/site/honorees/dix.html

Glossary

governess (GUH vur nuhss) A woman who teaches and trains children especially in a private home.

humane (hyoo MAYN) Kind and charitable.

insane (in SAYN) Mentally ill, suffering from a sickness of the mind.

legislature (LEJ iss LAY chur) A group of people who have the power to make or change laws for a country or state.

mental illness (MEN tuhl IL nuhss) A disease or sickness of the mind.

spinsters (SPIN sturz) Women who have never been married.

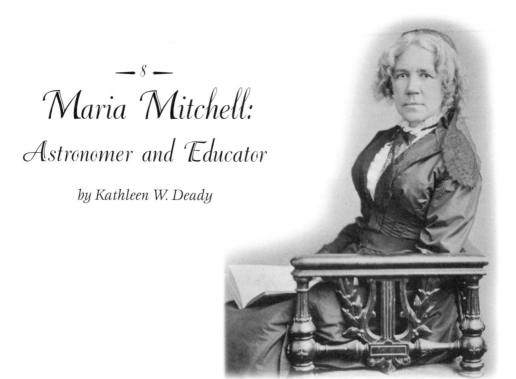

Maria Mitchell:
Astronomer and Educator

by Kathleen W. Deady

Maria left her parents' party. She grabbed her **cloak** and lantern and climbed through the attic to their rooftop **observatory**. Even at 29, she loved watching the stars as much as she had when she was a child.

Maria focused her telescope. Soon, she was sweeping the sky. She knew the stars and planets very well. For years, she had been looking and measuring and recording. She practically had the sky memorized.

Suddenly she stopped. What was that tiny, blurry light near the North Star? It had never been there before. There was only one explanation. It made her heart pound. Could she be looking at something that no one else in the world had ever seen?

· · · · ໑໑ · · · ·

Maria Mitchell was born on August 1, 1818 on Nantucket Island off the coast of Massachusetts. Like most people on the island, her parents were **Quakers.** They thought learning was very important. Quakers believed that girls should have the same education as boys.

Maria was eager to learn. Much of her education came from what her father taught her. He encouraged her interest in science. He was an amateur **astronomer** and had a rooftop observatory. Maria spent much of her time with her father studying the night sky.

Maria was very good at math. When she was 12, she watched a **lunar eclipse** with her father. Together, they recorded the exact moment of the eclipse. They used a **chronometer** to count the seconds.

Maria did attend some school. When her father opened a school, she attended it for a while. Later, she attended Cyrus Peirce's School for Young Ladies.

At 18, Maria worked as a librarian. She read many books and became very well educated. She also continued to study the night sky.

Then, on October 1, 1847, Maria noticed a blurry light near the North Star. She realized it was a comet. The King of Denmark had offered a gold medal to anyone who discovered a new comet using a telescope. Maria received the medal. She was soon famous.

Life quickly changed for Maria. She became well respected around the world. Scientific organizations elected her their first woman member. Scientists asked her to work with them.

Maria also traveled more to attend scientific meetings. Away from Nantucket, she was surprised to find a lack of respect for women. Women were not encouraged to become educated. They did not have many of the same rights as men.

TIDBITS

Nantucket was a major whaling seaport. One of her father's jobs was to take care of the instruments used on the ships. At 14, Maria could adjust a ship's instruments and knew how they worked.

•◆•

Maria was the first woman astronomer in the United States.

•◆•

The Vassar Observatory had a 12-inch telescope. At that time, it was the third best telescope in the country.

TIDBITS

The Women's Congress formed to help women gain equal rights, including the right to vote and own property. Other women attending included Susan B. Anthony and Elizabeth Cady Stanton.

•◆•

Maria worked hard for women's education. "I believe in women even more than I do in astronomy," she once said.

•◆•

Mitchell crater on the moon is named after Maria.

Maria believed strongly that this situation needed to change.

In 1865, Vassar College asked Maria to teach astronomy. Maria was the first woman professor at the school. Maria's students loved her. She made her classes interesting and got the students excited about learning.

Maria also worked for women to have the same rights as men. In 1873, she helped plan the first Women's Congress. This new group felt women should be able to vote and own property. Two years later, Maria became president of the group. She encouraged women to become educated and enter professions.

In 1888, Maria retired from teaching. She died the following year. After she died, her friends founded the Maria Mitchell Association on Nantucket. They wanted to honor Maria and her work. They offered programs to help people study the sciences.

Maria was a scientist who always questioned. She was a beloved educator. And she was a woman who worked to open doors for other women.

A painting of Maria Mitchell done by H. Dassel in 1851.

Timeline: Maria Mitchell

1818	August 1, born to Quaker parents Lydia Coleman and William Mitchell, the third of ten children in the family.
1834	Becomes an assistant teacher at Cyrus Peirce's School for Young Ladies.
1836	At 18 years old, accepts job as first librarian at the Nantucket Atheneum Library. Reads many books in math, languages, and navigation.
1847	October 1, discovers a new comet using a telescope, receives award, becomes world famous.
1848	Becomes first woman member in the American Academy of the Arts and Sciences. Remains the only woman until 1943.
1849	Accepts job with U.S. Nautical Almanac Office. Uses math to make tables showing the positions of Venus.
1850	Becomes first woman member in Association for the Advancement of Science.
1856	Travels to Europe. Becomes the first woman allowed inside the Vatican Observatory in Rome. However, she is not allowed to stay after dark to use the telescope.
1861	Maria's mother dies. Maria and her father move to Lynn, Massachusetts to live with her married sister.
1865	Accepts position as professor of Astronomy at Vassar College. Vassar is a new college in Poughkeepsie, NY, one of the first colleges for women in the country.
1869	Maria's father dies.
1873	Helps plan and attends first meeting of the Women's Congress to work for women's rights. The group becomes The Association for the Advancement of Women (AAW).
1875	Is elected President of AAW. Serves for two years. Leads annual meetings, encourages women to become educated and enter all professions.
1888	Retires from Vassar because of poor health, returns to Massachusetts.
1889	Dies on June 3 at age 71 of a brain disease.
1902	The Maria Mitchell Association is founded on Nantucket Island.
1994	Inducted into National Women's Hall of Fame.

Learn More about Maria Mitchell and Astronomy

- Driscoll, Michael. *A Child's Introduction to the Night Sky: The Story of the Stars, Planets, and Constellations--and How You Can Find Them in the Sky.* Black Dog & Leventhal Publishers, 2004.

- Einspruch, Andrew. *Mysteries of the Universe: How Astronomers Explore Space.* National Geographic Society, 2006.

- Gormley, Beatrice. *Maria Mitchell: The Soul of an Astronomer.* William E. Eerdmans Publishing Company, 1995.

- McPhearson, Stephanie Sammartino. *Rooftop Astronomer: A Story about Maria Mitchell.* Carolrhoda Books, 1990.

- Way, Jennifer. *Exploring Comets.* Power Kids Press, 2007.

Websites:

- Unitarian Universalist Historical Society:
  http://www25.uua.org/uuhs/duub/articles/mariamitchell.html

- Distinguished Women of Past and Present:
  http://www.distinguishedwomen.com/biographies/mitchell.html

Glossary

astronomer (uh STRON uh mur) A person who studies the stars, planets, and space.

chronometer (kruh NAW muh tur) A device that measures time very accurately.

cloak (KLOHK) A loose coat with no sleeves.

lunar eclipse (LOO nur i KLIPS) When the earth comes between the sun and the moon so that all or part of the moon's light is blocked out.

observatory (uhb ZUR vuh tore ee) A building containing telescopes and other instruments for studying the sky.

Quaker (KWAY kur) A member of the Society of Friends, a Christian group founded in 1650 that prefers simple religious services and opposes war.

— 9 —
Lucy Larcom:
Millgirl, Teacher, Poet

by Kathleen W. Deady

Seven-year-old Lucy played in the attic with her older brother John.

"Let's write poetry," John suggested. John soon tired of writing, but Lucy thought it was fun. She wrote about the storm outside.

> One summer day, said little Jane,
>
> We were walking down a shady lane,
>
> When suddenly the wind blew high,
>
> And the red lightening flashed in the sky.

Later the family insisted she recite her words. Lucy thought they sounded silly. But in writing them, she had started something deep inside. Poetry would become something she could not live without.

· · · · ⟲ · · · ·

Lucy Larcom was born in Beverly, Massachusetts on March 5, 1824. She was the ninth of ten children in a family that included eight girls.

TIDBITS

The Lowell mill girls received the highest wages paid to any women in America. They were paid from $1.85 to $3.00 a week.

Some mill girls sent money home to help their parents. Most, however, earned the money for school or new clothes. They were the first women to have their own bank accounts.

People around the country read the *Lowell Offering*. Lucy became the best-known writer in the magazine.

The oldest two girls were from her father's first wife, who had died in childbirth.

Lucy was a cheerful and bright child. She learned her alphabet at two years old, and was reading by two and a half. In church, Lucy often memorized the **hymns.** She then recited them to her family. She loved the rhythm and the sound of the words.

Childhood was a happy and free time for Lucy. She loved exploring the natural world around their home. Then, when she was seven, her life changed suddenly. Lucy's father died. Her mother struggled to raise their large family alone.

In 1835, the family moved to Lowell. Her mother ran a **dormitory** for girls who worked in the mills. At first, Lucy went to school. Soon, like her older sisters, Lucy began working in the mills to help support the family.

Lucy started as a **doffer**, replacing **bobbins** on the looms. Later, she worked on the looms and as a bookkeeper. The hours were long, often 60 to 75 hours a week. The machines were very noisy and lint filled the air. Over time, Lucy was tired and tense. She often had headaches and very little energy.

To make the days more pleasant, Lucy cut poems out of newspapers and hung them on the walls near her loom. She dreamed of getting a **formal** education. In the little spare time she had, Lucy took classes and read many books.

Some of the mill girls began a magazine called the *Lowell Offering*. They published their own stories, poems and letters. Lucy's poems were in almost every issue.

In 1846, Lucy left the mills and moved west to Illinois. She taught school for three years. She then went to Monticello Female **Seminary.** Lucy graduated in 1852 and returned home to Massachusetts.

To support herself, Lucy taught at Wheaton Female Seminary. She wrote when she had time. Slowly, she began publishing in national magazines. Lucy was a good teacher. However, she never really liked the demands on her time. She longed for the freedom to write more. Lucy's health suffered. By 1862, she left teaching.

Lucy finally felt free. She was determined to support herself by writing. In the coming years, Lucy wrote eight books of poetry. Her work was published in many collections and well-known magazines. She also edited a children's magazine, *Our Young Folks,* for eight years.

Lucy was well respected as a poet. She wrote of many things, including nature, religion, and politics. Today, she is most remembered for her **autobiography.** *A New England Girlhood* is the story of her years as a mill girl. She died on April 17, 1893 of heart disease.

TIDBITS

Lucy met the poet John Greenleaf Whittier while at the mills. He noticed her poems in the *Lowell Offering.* In the beginning, he often guided her writing. They remained life-long friends.

•◆•

Lucy's millwork affected the rest of her life. She hated noise and being confined by small spaces or by rules.

•◆•

Lucy felt conflicted all her life. She held jobs to support herself. But she always wanted to write, which she truly felt was her calling.

Children were often hired as "doffers." Their job was to replace full spools of threads with empty spools.

Timeline: Lucy Larcom

1824 ➤ March 5, Lucy is born in Beverly, Massachusetts to Benjamin Larcom, a retired sea captain, and Lois Barrett Larcom, a homemaker. Her siblings include Charlotte (1806) and Adelaide (1810) from her father's first marriage, as well as Benjamin (1814), Louisa (1815), Emeline (1817), Jonathan (1818), Abigail (1820), Lydia (1822), and later, Octavia (1827).

1832 ➤ Father dies, Lucy's mother struggles to raise their large family alone.

1835 ➤ Family moves to Lowell. Mother takes job as supervisor of a dormitory for the women working in the mills.

1840 ➤ Lucy and other mill girls start the *Lowell Offering*. This literary magazine publishes fiction stories, poems, and letters.

1843 ➤ Poet John Greenleaf Whittier notices one of Lucy's poems in the *Lowell Offering*. They develop a life-long friendship.

1846 ➤ Lucy leaves the mills and moves west to the Illinois prairie with her sister Emeline and her new husband.

1849 ➤ Enters Monticello Seminary in Godfrey, Illinois. This same year, Lucy's work is mentioned in *Female Poets of America*.

1852 ➤ Graduates from Monticello Seminary, returns to Massachusetts.

1854 ➤ Wins prize for "Call to Kansas," her poem about settlement efforts in Kansas.

1854–1862 ➤ Teaches at Wheaton Female Seminary, in Norton, Massachusetts, now called Wheaton College. Teaches literature, philosophy, history and botany. Also founds school newspaper. Writes when she has time, begins selling to national magazines.

1865–c1873 ➤ Becomes Assistant Editor, then Editor of children's magazine, *Our Young Folks*. During this time, publishes widely in many well-known magazines, including *The Atlantic Monthly, Harper's New Monthly Magazine,* and *New England Monthly Magazine*.

1889 ➤ Writes *A New England Girlhood*, a book about her experiences working in the Lowell mills growing up.

1893 ➤ April 17, dies of heart disease at 69 years old.

NOTE: c1873 means about or around 1873

Learn More about Lucy Larcom and the Life of Mill Girls

- Flanagan, Alice K. *The Lowell Mill Girls.* Compass Point Books, 2006.
- McCully, Emily Arnold. *The Bobbin Girl.* Dial, 1996

Websites:

- Larcom, Lucy, 1824-1893:
  http://www.alexanderstreet2.com/CWLDLive/BIOS/A40BIO.html
- Larcom Family Tree:
  http://www.larcomfamilytree.com/lucy/index.html
- "Millgirl" Writer Lucy Larcom Dies:
  http://www.massmoments.org/moment.cfm?mid = 116

Glossary

autobiography (AW toh bye OG ruh fee) A book in which the author tells the story of his or her life.

botany (BOT uh nee) The scientific study of plants.

doffer (DOF uhr) A person whose job it was to remove full spools of thread on a weaving machine and replace them with empty spools. In the 1800s this job was often done by children.

dormitory (DOR muh tor ee) A building with many separate sleeping rooms.

formal (FOR muhl) Official.

hymn (HIM) A song of praise to God.

seminary (SEM uh NER ee) An old-fashioned word for college. A school that trains students to become teachers.

— 10 —
Louisa May Alcott:
Writer, Reformer, Celebrity

by Sally Wilkins

*L*ouisa dropped into a chair at the end of the converted hotel ballroom. For hours she had changed bandages and emptied bedpans. "Tell us a story, Miss Alcott," the wounded soldiers begged. Each night Louisa reported interesting things she had seen in the Washington streets. She shared memories of her childhood. Her tales helped pass the long hours. The soldiers loved her.

After five weeks Louisa contracted **typhoid.** The doctor ordered her to bed. For days she tossed in a raging fever. Louisa's father took her home on the train. Louisa survived, but her brief job as a Civil War nurse changed her life.

· · · · ๑ · · · ·

Louisa May Alcott was born November 29, 1832 in Germantown, Pennsylvania. Her family moved to Boston when she was two.

Louisa's father, Bronson, was a **Transcendentalist.** He opened a new school in Boston. Boys and girls, black and white all learned in the same classroom. Louisa loved the lessons, games, and stories.

Bronson never made very much money. To survive, Louisa's mother, Abba, took in sewing and laundry. Louisa and her sister, Anna, made sheets. Abba's relatives and their friend Ralph Waldo Emerson helped pay the rent. The Alcotts moved often.

When Louisa was eleven, Bronson moved the family to a **utopian** farm, Fruitlands. Bronson and his friends talked more than they farmed. There was not enough food or firewood. After six months, Abba told Bronson to choose between his family and his philosopher friends. That was the end of Fruitlands. Abba went to work. She became the first paid **social worker** in Massachusetts. Anna and Louisa taught and sewed. Younger sister Lizzie kept house. May, the youngest, was in school.

Louisa loved stories. She wrote and acted in plays with her sisters. At fifteen she had a job teaching Mr. Emerson's daughter, Ellen. Louise made a book about garden fairies for Ellen. She told her mother she would become a writer and support the family. In the 1850s Louisa sold several "blood and thunder" stories using a **pen name**. Magazine readers loved these wild romantic tales. Then came the Civil War. Louisa went to be a war nurse.

As Louisa recovered from typhoid, she wrote about the soldiers. A Boston newspaper paid for the stories. Readers wanted news about the war. Two companies offered to publish *Hospital Sketches* as a book.

Soon many publishers asked Louisa for stories. When she was writing Louisa forgot to eat or sleep. She would work for weeks, then collapse.

TIDBITS

Louisa loved to act in plays, especially for charitable causes. She wrote and performed a one-woman show based on characters of Charles Dickens.

The character of Jo's friend Laurie Lawrence in *Little Women* was based on a young Polish refugee Louisa met in while traveling in Europe as a lady's companion.

Fifty thousand copies of the American edition of *Little Men* were sold before the book was published.

•◆•

Once a young bookseller on the train to New York tried to convince Louisa to buy the latest hit: her own *Under the Lilacs.*

•◆•

Louisa was the first woman to register to vote in Concord, Massachusetts in 1879 (41 years before the 19th Amendment gave women the vote across the United States).

One of Louisa's publishers asked her to write a book "for girls." In *Little Women* Louisa turned her sisters into Meg, Beth and Amy and herself into Jo. *Little Women* was instantly popular. Boys and adults loved Louisa's "book for girls," too.

At last Louisa had enough money to support the family. She gave her mother a comfortable room, sent her father on lecture tours, and took her sister May to Europe.

Louisa's readers begged for more books. In *Little Men* and *Jo's Boys* Louisa created the school her father had imagined. Louisa's readers didn't know they were learning about women's rights, **temperance,** and educational reform. They just knew her books were fun.

Louisa provided for Anna's sons and made a home for May's daughter, Lulu. She nursed her mother, sisters, and father when they were sick. One raw March day in 1888, Louisa went to check on her father. On the way home she caught pneumonia. Louisa and Bronson died just two days apart.

"Orchard House" was the Alcotts' home in Concord, Massachusetts.

Timeline: Louisa May Alcott

1832	➤	November 29, Louisa May Alcott is born Germantown, Pennsylvania, second daughter of Amos Bronson Alcott and Abigail Sewall May.
1834	➤	Bronson opens experimental Temple School in Boston.
1839	➤	Temple school closes after scandal over **racial integration** and sex education.
1843	➤	The family lives at Fruitlands, a Utopian **Commune**.
1847	➤	Louisa writes *Flower Fables* as a gift for Ellen Emerson. It would be published in 1854.
1850	➤	Louisa sees escaped slaves recaptured in Boston under the Fugitive Slave Law.
1852	➤	First magazine story, "The Rival Painters," published.
1858	➤	Sister Lizzie dies just before Alcotts move to Orchard House in Concord.
1860	➤	The wife and daughter of executed abolitionist John Brown board with the Alcotts at Orchard House. Louisa's poem about Brown is published in *The Liberator*.
1861	➤	War Between the States (The Civil War) begins.
1862	➤	Joins Army nurse volunteers. Works under Dorothea Dix at Union Hospital in Washington, DC.
1863	➤	*Hospital Sketches* serialized in *The Commonwealth*, then published as a book by James Redpath.
1865	➤	Louisa travels to Europe as a companion to Anna Weld.
1867	➤	Agrees to edit and write for *Merry's Museum*, a top children's magazine.
1868	➤	Writes a "new" kind of story for girls, *Little Women,* for publisher Thomas Niles.
1869	➤	*Little Women* (Part II) celebrates Anna (Meg's) wedding to John Pratt (Brook).
1871	➤	Visiting Italy with May, Louisa writes *Little Men* to provide an income to her sister, Anna, and her sons. It is published in England in May and in Boston in June.
1877	➤	Louisa's mother Abba is in declining health. She dies November 25.
1879	➤	May's infant daughter Lulu comes to Boston to live with Louisa after May dies.
1888	➤	Bronson Alcott dies March 4, Louisa dies March 6. Both are buried at Sleepy Hollow in Concord, Massachusetts.

Learn More About Louisa May Alcott and Her Times

- Ditchfield, Christin. *Louisa May Alcott: Author of Little Women.* Scholastic, Inc., 2005.

- Ford, Carin T. *Daring Women of the Civil War.* Enslow Publishers, 2004.

- Graves, Kerry A., editor. *The Girlhood Diary of Louisa May Alcott, 1843-1846: Writings of a Young Author*. Blue Earth Books, 2001.

- Silverthorne, Elizabeth. *Louisa May Alcott (Who Wrote That?)*. Chelsea House, 2002.

Website:

- Official Website of Orchard House museum: www.louisamayalcott.org/

- Biography of Louisa from Unitarian Universalist Society: http://www25.uua.org/uuhs/duub/articles/louisamayalcott.html

Glossary

commune (KOM yoon) A group of people who live together and share things with each other.

pen name (pen naym) A made up name used by an author instead of his or her real name.

racial integration (RAY shuhl in tuh GRAY shuhn) Making facilities or organizations open to people of all races and ethnic groups.

social worker (SOH shuhl WUR kur) A person who provides help, services, or activities to the poor.

temperance (TEM prinss) A movement that urged people not to drink alcoholic beverages.

transcendentalist (TRAN sen DEN tuhl ist) A person who believes that feelings and the spirititual are more important than what can be seen or touched.

typhoid fever (TYE foid FEE vur) A serious disease caused by germs in food or water. The symptoms include a high fever and diarrhea and can lead to death.

utopian (yoo TOH pee uhn) One who believes a perfect society can be created.

Isabella Stewart Gardner: Patron of the Arts

by Andrea Murphy

Did you see that? Did you see what that woman has on her head?
It's scandalous!

Isabella settled into her seat. The Boston Symphony Orchestra was about to play, but all eyes were on Isabella. As usual, she was dressed exquisitely. Except for the white headband wrapped around her red hair. Red letters ran across the band. They said, *Oh you Red Sox!*

The crowd buzzed with outrage. Isabella simply smiled.

Isabella Stewart was born in New York City on April 14, 1840. Her father, David, and her mother, Adelia, were very wealthy. Isabella had one sister and two brothers.

Isabella's happy life was shaken around 1853. Her sister Adelia died. Her parents moved the family to France. Isabella went to **finishing school** in Paris.

TIDBITS

When the Stewarts returned to America, Isabella met John Lowell Gardner, Jr. His friends called him Jack. The two soon fell in love, and were married in 1860.

Isabella and Jack settled in Boston. In June 1863, Isabella gave birth to John Lowell Gardner III. Isabella adored her son, who she called Jackie.

Isabella's joy ended in March 1864. Baby Jackie died of **pneumonia**. For two long years Isabella **grieved**. She was depressed and ill. Her doctors told her to travel to heal her sorrow.

Isabella and Jack went to Europe. When they returned to America, Isabella was healthy and happy.

By this time, Isabella was known as Mrs. Jack. She was determined to live her life as she pleased. Women were expected to be proper ladies. Mrs. Jack was outrageous.

She drank beer. She went to baseball games and boxing matches. She drove her car too fast. She had two diamonds fastened to springs and wore them like **antennae**.

People started telling wild stories about her. One rumor had Isabella walking a lion on a leash. Isabella used to say, "Don't spoil a good story by telling the truth." Boston society rejected her.

She became friends with artists, **suffragists**, and professors. Author Henry James turned her into characters for his books. Artist John Singer Sargent painted her picture.

Isabella threw fantastic parties. She became the talk of the town. It didn't matter that society people rejected her. The magazine *Town Topics* called her "Boston's most cherished institution."

Isabella and Jack started collecting art work. When Isabella's father died in 1891, he left her a great fortune. She used this money to buy even more art. She collected important paintings, sculptures, silver, **tapestries**, rare books and more. Isabella put together one of America's first great art collections. Isabella and Jack decided to build Fenway Court.

Jack died in 1898. Isabella went ahead with their plans. Fenway Court would hold her magnificent collection. She designed the building to look like an Italian palace.

In 1901, she moved into an apartment on the 4th floor. Fenway Court was opened to invited guests on January 1, 1903.

At first, Isabella's museum home was open only 20 days a year. Today it is open year round. Isabella ordered that all the art work must remain exactly as she arranged it. If it is moved or changed in any way, the entire collection must be sold. The museum appears much the same today as it did the day it opened.

Isabella died at Fenway Court on June 17, 1924.

Today, Fenway Court is called the Isabella Stuart Gardner Museum.

TIDBITS

People named "Isabella" are admitted to the Isabella Stewart Gardner Museum free of charge.

In 1990, two thieves dressed as police officers overpowered the guards at the Isabella Stewart Gardner Museum. They stole 13 works of art valued at around 300 million dollars. Despite a 5 million dollar reward, the art work has yet to be recovered. It was the largest art **heist** in modern history.

Timeline: Isabella Stewart Gardner

1840 ➤ April 14, Isabella is born the first of four children to David and Adelia (Smith) Stewart in New York City.

c1853 ➤ Her 11-year old sister Adelia dies.

1856–1858 ➤ Isabella and her family live in Paris, France.

1860 ➤ April 10, marries John Lowell Gardner, Jr. at Grace Church in New York City.

1863 ➤ June, her only child, John "Jackie" Lowell Gardner III, is born.

1864 ➤ March, Jackie dies of pneumonia.

1875 ➤ Isabella and Jack adopt Jack's 3 orphaned nephews.

1891 ➤ Upon her father's death, Isabella inherits a fortune. She uses it to expand her growing art collection.

1898 ➤ December 10, husband Jack dies.

1901 ➤ Isabella moves into Fenway Court.

1903 ➤ January 1, Isabella opens Fenway Court to her friends. The Boston Symphony Orchestra plays for the event.

February 23, Isabella opens Fenway Court to the public.

1919 ➤ Isabella suffers the first of several strokes.

1924 ➤ June 17, Isabella dies and is buried between her husband and son in Mount Auburn Cemetery in Cambridge, Massachusetts.

1990 ➤ March 18, the Isabella Stewart Gardner Museum is robbed. The art heist is the largest in modern history.

NOTE: c1853 means about or around 1853

Learn More About Isabella Stewart Gardner, Great Art, and Boston:

- Balliett, Blue and Helquist, Brett. ***Chasing Vermeer***. Scholastic Press, 2004.
- Chong, Alan (Editor). ***Eye of the Beholder: Masterpieces from the Isabella Stewart Gardner Museum***. Beacon Press, 2003.
- Muhlberger, Richard. ***What Makes a Rembrandt A Rembrandt?*** Viking Juvenile, 2002.
- Boroson, Melinda R. ***86 Years: The Legend of the Boston Red Sox***. Brown House Books, 2005.

Websites:

- The Isabella Stewart Gardner Museum Website: www.gardnermuseum.org
- Explore "Everything Art": www.smithsonianeducation.org/students
- Find places to visit in Boston: http://www.bpl.org/kids/bostoninfo.htm
- Learn about Isabella Stewart Gardner's favorite baseball team: http://mlb.mlb.com/mlb/kids/index.jsp?c_id=bos

Glossary

antennae (an TEN ee) Feelers on the head of an insect.

finishing school (FIN ish ing SKOOL) An additional year of school usually consisting of a special program of study.

grieved (GREEVD) Felt very sad because someone you loved has died.

heist (HEYEST) The act of stealing; a theft.

pneumonia (noo MOH nyuh) A serious disease that causes the lungs to fill with liquid and makes breathing difficult.

scandalous (SKAN duhl uhs) Disgraceful or dishonorable.

suffragists (SUHF rij ists) People who believed in giving women the right to vote.

tapestries (TAP uh streez) Heavy cloths with pictures or patterns woven into them.

— 12 —
Ellen Swallow Richards:
America's First Woman Chemist

by M. Lu Major

The news was shocking. Ellen Swallow's father had been hit by a train. Ellen and her mother did their best to care for him. But his wounds were too severe and he died four days later.

Just weeks before, Ellen had begun studying at the Massachusetts Institute of Technology. She was the college's only woman student. Most of the professors did not want women at the school. If she did not return soon, MIT might think women had no place there.

But Ellen was an only child. Her mother would be alone. Should Ellen leave college?

· · · · ⟳ · · · ·

Ellen Swallow was born in 1842 in Dunstable, Massachusetts. When Ellen was 16, the Swallows moved to Westford, Massachusetts so Ellen could attend Westford Academy. After graduation, Ellen worked for six years to earn the money for college. She worked in a store, tutored Latin students, and taught school. She also educated herself by going to lectures and reading.

Vassar College admitted Ellen in 1868. In two years, she earned a **bachelor's degree** in chemistry. Women chemists were a new idea. No one would hire Ellen. She applied to study at the Massachusetts Institute of Technology (MIT). Women never had been accepted there. The college awarded Ellen a full scholarship. It was not the honor it seemed. If anyone complained, the school could say Ellen was only a guest.

Weeks after she began her term, Ellen's father died. For months she traveled back and forth to MIT every day. She did not want her mother to be alone. Ellen's days were long. It would have been easy to quit, but Ellen wanted to stay in school. She won over her teachers by offering her help. "Perhaps the fact… that I …clean up and … sew things… is winning me stronger **allies** than anything else," she wrote.

In 1869, Massachusetts opened the first State Board of Health. The Board asked MIT to test the state's water. Ellen did most of the testing. She worked seven days a week. She checked samples while keeping up her own studies. In 1873, Ellen received two more degrees. She began to teach at MIT. She opened the Women's Laboratory.

Ellen's most important work used chemistry to create healthier homes. She called this science *Euthenics*. Ellen examined inventions like gas heat and vacuum cleaners. She tested different types of soap. She studied **nutrition**. Today, this science is called **Home Economics**

These studies led to important projects. At the New England Kitchen, Ellen developed recipes that were **consistent**. Healthy

TIDBITS

Ellen hated to waste time. She even knitted as she walked up the stairs to her room at Vassar College.

⋅━⋅

After college, Ellen joined the Society to Encourage Studies at Home. She wrote science lessons students could use. The lessons came with microscopes and other instruments.

As hard as Ellen worked for the education of women, she did not support the Suffragettes. She wrote in her diary: "I think the women have a lot to learn before they are fit to vote."

In 1875, Ellen married MIT professor Robert H. Richards. They honeymooned in Nova Scotia. Robert's entire mining class went along because this was a working trip. Ellen worked as the class's **botanist**.

food was made in a clean kitchen. She opened another kitchen called the Rumford Kitchen. This one was at the World's Columbian Exhibition in Chicago. In two months, more than 10,000 people ate there. The menu showed the nutrition facts for each dish, just as labels do today.

The Boston School Committee asked Ellen to study school lunches. Students bought lunch from school janitors or nearby shops. The School Committee wanted children to eat healthy food. Ellen's work paved the way for the school lunch programs.

Chemistry was not Ellen's only interest. She also kept weather maps. She studied minerals and plants.

Ellen taught at MIT until her death in 1911. She spoke all over the country. She wrote dozens of books. But for all her work, MIT would not give its highest degree, a **doctorate**, to a woman. Today, though, MIT honors her memory. The school awards women professors the Ellen Swallow Richards Professorship.

A photo of the tiny Rumford Kitchen at the World's Columbian Exhibition in Chicago, 1893.

Timeline: Ellen Swallow Richards

1842 ➤ December 3, Ellen is born in Dunstable, Massachusetts to farmer and teacher Peter Swallow and his wife, Fanny.

1859 ➤ Peter Swallow sells the family farm. The Swallows move to Westford, MA so Ellen can attend the town's academy. Peter Swallow opens a store.

1863 ➤ The family moves to Littleton, MA, where Peter Swallow opens a larger store.

1865–1866 ➤ Ellen works in the store, teaches, tutors, and prepares to attend Vassar College in New York.

1868 ➤ Enters Vassar College as a special student.

1870 ➤ Graduates from Vassar. Ellen receives a Bachelor of Science degree in chemistry.

1871 ➤ January, is the first woman admitted to MIT.

March, her father dies four days after being hit by a train.

1873 ➤ Ellen becomes the first woman to graduate from MIT. She receives a second Bachelor of Science degree in chemistry.

Ellen also submits a **thesis** on the chemical analysis of iron ore to Vassar College and receives a Master's degree.

1875 ➤ June 4, marries Robert H. Richards, MIT professor of mining engineering.

1876 ➤ January, creates science lessons for Study at Home.

November, opens the Women's Laboratory at MIT.

1879 ➤ Becomes the first woman elected to active membership in the American Institute of Mining Engineers for her work with ores and metals.

1884 ➤ Is appointed instructor in Sanitary Chemistry at MIT. She shows how to keep drinking water clean and food preparation safe.

1886 ➤ MIT establishes the first separate laboratory for the study of sanitary chemistry.

1888 ➤ Ellen helps to establish a new part of the Study at Home group, Correspondence University, to provide graduate studies for women.

1890 ➤ Organizes the New England Kitchen.

1893 ➤ Runs the Rumford Kitchen at the World's Columbian Exposition.

1894 ➤ The New England Kitchen begins an experimental school lunch program.

1911 ➤ Ellen dies at home from heart disease.

Read More About Ellen Swallow Richards and Women in Chemistry

- Kahn, Jetty. *Women in Chemistry Careers (Capstone Short Biographies)*. Capstone Press, 2000.

- Krensky, Stephen. *What's the Big Idea? Four Centuries of Innovation in Boston.* Charlesbridge Publications, 2008.

- Stille, Darlene R. *Extraordinary Women Scientists (Extraordinary People)*. Children's Press, 1995.

- Vare, Ethlie Ann. *Adventurous Spirit: A Story About Ellen Swallow Richards (Creative Minds Biographies)*. Carolrhoda Books, 1992.

Websites:

- Read about some of today's most interesting women in chemistry: http://www.chemheritage.org/women_chemistry/

- A short biography of Ellen H. Swallow Richards: http://www.astr.ua.edu/4000WS/RICHARDS.html

Glossary

allies (AL eyez) People or countries that support one another.

bachelor's degree (BACH uh lurz di GREE) The diploma received after 4 years of college study.

botanist (BOT uh nist) A scientist who studies plants.

consistent (kuhn SISS tuhnt) Always behaving in the same manner; predictable.

doctorate (DOK tuh ruht) The highest degree given by a university.

Home Economics (HOME ek uh NOM iks) The science of homemaking.

nutrition (noo TRISH uhn) The way the body takes in and uses food.

thesis (THEE siss) An idea to be debated or proved. A person who is working towards a doctorate usually must write a thesis on the topic he or she studied.

— 13 —
Mary Eliza Mahoney:
First Black Professional Nurse

by Diane Mayr

Mary Mahoney applied to nursing school at New England Hospital for Women and Children. She was two years older than the 31 year cut-off age. She had been working at the hospital for several years. The doctors in charge knew she was a good worker. They decided to accept her at the school.

The odds were against Mary succeeding. She was older. She was black. No black woman had ever graduated from a school of nursing. The training would be hard. She would need to work and study 16 hours a day. Seven days a week. For 16 months straight. Would she keep up? Would she graduate?

· · · · ೧၅ · · · ·

Mary Eliza Mahoney was born on May 7, 1845, in a part of Boston called Dorchester. She was the oldest of three children.

The Civil War broke out when Mary was sixteen. There was a great need for nurses during the Civil War. She became interested in nursing.

At the time in which she lived, black people were called "colored." They were often treated poorly. Many black women had to take **menial** jobs. Hospital stays were not common in the 1800s. Relatives hired black people to care for the sick at home.

In 1862, women opened New England Hospital for Women and Children. Women had not been welcomed in the field of medicine. At the new hospital they could study to become doctors. Women would be trained as nurses.

Mahoney went to New England Hospital to work. She cleaned, cooked, and did washing. She wanted more. She applied to the hospital's nursing school and was accepted. The course of study was hard. Students attended lectures. They worked with doctors and patients every day. Their duties included working at night. Those who could not keep up were told to leave. Eighteen women had been accepted at the school. Only Mary and three other women from that class graduated. Mary became America's first black **professional** nurse.

After graduation she went to work as a private nurse. Private nurses stayed with a patient 24 hours a day. Some families expected the nurse to do other jobs, too. These included washing clothes or cleaning the house. A private nurse didn't have much time of her own. Perhaps that is why Mary never married.

Mary Mahoney's name was listed in a Boston **directory** of nurses. She worked for many people around Boston. In the directory they wrote that Mary was "an excellent nurse." Good

recommendations meant she could get more jobs. Families hired her again and again. Mary traveled far to care for her patients. She went to New Jersey and North Carolina.

Mahoney wanted black nurses and white nurses to be treated equally. She and several others started a group. They called themselves the National Association of Graduate Colored Nurses. They worked to support and educate black nurses.

Later in life, Mary moved to New York for a short time. She was director of the Howard Colored Orphan **Asylum**. The asylum took in black children who did not have parents to care for them.

Mary Mahoney was active in nursing until her death at age 81. She died at New England Hospital for Women and Children. It was the hospital where she had trained as a nurse.

The gravestone designed for Mary in 1973.

TIDBITS

Women gained the right to vote in 1920. Mary was said to have been one of the first women to register and vote in Boston.

• ◆ •

When Mary died in 1926, she was buried with a simple gravestone. In 1973, two nurses who had been awarded the Mary Mahoney Award designed a new monument for Mary's grave.

• ◆ •

In 1976, 50 years after she died, Mary Eliza Mahoney was elected to the Nursing Hall of Fame.

Timeline: Mary Eliza Mahoney

1845 ➤ May 7, is born in Dorchester, a part of Boston, Massachusetts. Her parents, Charles Mahoney and Mary Jane Stewart Mahoney, had moved there from North Carolina.

1860–1865 ➤ The Civil War is fought. The need for nurses grows.

1862 ➤ New England Hospital for Women and Children opens. One of its purposes is to train women as nurses.

1865–1878 ➤ Mary works in the Boston area, including several years at New England Hospital for Women and Children.

1878 ➤ March 18, enrolls in nursing school at New England Hospital for Women and Children. Her training lasts 16 months.

1879 ➤ August 1, graduates with a certificate of nursing. She becomes the first African-American professional nurse.

1879–c1910 ➤ Works as a private nurse. Also works to advance other black women in the field of nursing.

1908 ➤ The National Association of Graduate Colored Nurses (NAGCN) is formed. Mary is later honored for her service and is given a life-time membership.

1911 ➤ Mary moves to King's Park, New York, to become director of the Howard Colored Orphan Asylum. She stays for 1½ years until she retires.

1926 ➤ January 4, dies of cancer at New England Hospital for Women and Children. She is buried in Everett, Massachusetts.

1936 ➤ In her honor the NAGCN gives the first Mary Mahoney Award. The award is still given out today.

NOTE: c1910 means about or around 1910

Learn More About Mary Eliza Mahoney and Nursing

- Brandon, Karen. *Nurse. ("How Do I Become a...?" series).* Gale Group, 2005.

- Brill, Marlene T. *Nurses.* Lerner, 2005.

- Darraj, Susan M. *Mary Eliza Mahoney and the Legacy of African-American Nurses.* Chelsea House, 2005.

- Stille, Darlene R. *Extraordinary Women of Medicine.* Children's Press, 1997.

Websites:

- To learn more about nursing as a career:
  http://www.discovernursing.com/

- A history of New England Hospital for Women and Children and some of its women doctors and nurses:
  http://www.homeoint.org/cazalet/histo/newengland.htm

- Mary Mahoney is included with 5 other African-American pioneers of medicine:
  http://www.pbs.org/wgbh/amex/partners/early/e_pioneers.swf

- Download the "You Can Be A Nurse" coloring book:
  http://users.ipfw.edu/sternber/Colo

Glossary

asylum (uh SYE luhm) A safe place, where a person is given care.

calico (KAL i koh) Brightly printed cotton cloth.

directory (duh REK tuh ree) A listing of names and addresses.

menial (MEE nee uhl) Referring to work that does not require special training, or is done by servants.

professional (pruh FESH uh nuhl) One who has received special training and education.

recommendations (rek uh mend AY shunz) Statements made which suggest that a person's work is good.

—14—
Edith Wharton:
Writer

by Barbara J. Turner

 $\mathcal{L}$ ittle Edith grabbed a book from her father's library and ran to her mother's bedroom. She could not read, but she held the book open and paced about the room. Turning the pages, she spoke aloud and told herself the most interesting story.

Outside the door, Edith's mother tried to write everything down. It was strange, this 'making up' her daughter did. Still, one never knew what might become of it. She continued to write, wishing Edith would 'make up' a bit slower.

· · · · ᏜᎧ · · · ·

Edith Newbold Jones was born in New York City on January 24, 1862. Her parents, Lucretia and George, were very wealthy. She and her two older brothers grew up in a world of parties and travel.

Edith preferred books to parties. As a child, she made up stories and taught herself to read. As she grew older, she read the books in her father's library. By age fifteen, she had written a **novella.** Behind her back, people whispered about that strange Jones girl who always had her head in a book. Edith didn't care. She continued to write, and sold poems to *The Atlantic Monthly* and the *New York World.*

Edith's mother *did* care. She decided to stop the whispering. She took Edith out more and introduced her to 'the right people.' Soon, Edith was engaged, but the engagement didn't last. **Gossip columns** said Edith was too **intellectual,** and her ambition to be a writer was a '**grievous** fault.'

Edith married her brother's friend, Edward 'Teddy' Wharton, in 1884. They had little in common. She liked books and art. He liked sports and the outdoors.

While Teddy hunted and played golf, Edith wrote. She wrote *The Decoration of Houses,* and began selling stories to *Scribner's Magazine.* She traveled to Europe and spent time with other writers and artists. She wrote *The House of Mirth,* which became a best-seller.

As the years passed, Teddy began showing signs of mental illness. He stole $50,000 from Edith's **trust fund** and sold their home in Lenox, Massachusetts without her knowing about it. In 1913, Edith divorced him and moved to France.

By now, people knew who Edith Wharton was. They invited her to salons - gatherings of interesting people who talked about politics, art, and literature. But the world Edith loved did not last long.

World War I broke out. The Germans marched on Paris.

TIDBITS

As a child, Edith read to her deaf grandmother by shouting through her **ear trumpet**.

◦—◦—◦

In Germany with her family at age eight, Edith contracted typhoid fever. Because the Franco-Prussian war was going on, no doctors were available to see her. Edith almost died before a doctor was found: the Tsar of Russia's personal physician.

TIDBITS

Edith's mother did not allow her to read American children's books of her day. She said the children spoke bad English. They spoke it without the author knowing it!

◆◆

Edith was very generous to her friends. When author Henry James fell on hard times, Edith asked publisher Charles Scribner to give him an advance of $8,000 to write a new book. The money secretly came from Edith.

Edith opened a workroom where French women could make bandages and earn money to feed their children. She set up a **dispensary** and brought in doctors to help the sick and wounded. She founded homes for **refugee** children and elderly **invalids.** She called her friends for donations.

Edith wanted to do more. She knew Europe could not win the war without America's help. She used her connections to get close to the front lines where the fighting was the worst. She wrote about what she saw and sent it to *Scribner's*. They published her stories and eventually, America did join in the fighting and helped win the war.

When the war ended, Edith returned to her writing. In 1921, she was the first woman to win the **Pulitzer Prize** for fiction for her novel, *The Age of Innocence.* By the time she died on August 11, 1937, she had written over forty books.

Edith Wharton and lawyer Walter Berry with two officers at the front in France, 1915.

Timeline: Edith Wharton

1862	➤	January 24, Edith Newbold Jones is born in New York City.
1877	➤	Finishes her first novella, *Fast and Loose.*
1878	➤	*Verses,* a short book of poems is printed.
1882	➤	March 15, Edith's father dies.
		Becomes engaged to Harry Leyden Stevens. The engagement ends shortly after.
1885	➤	April 29, marries Edward 'Teddy' Wharton.
1890	➤	First story for *Scribner's Magazine*, "Mrs. Manstey's View," is published.
1897	➤	Writes *The Decoration of Houses* with her interior designer, Ogden Codman.
1899	➤	Tours Italy and Switzerland with French novelist Paul Bourget.
1902	➤	Moves into *The Mount* - the home she and Teddy built in Lenox, MA.
1905	➤	January, *The House of Mirth* is serialized in *Scribner's Magazine* for eleven months and published as a book in October. It becomes a best-seller.
1909	➤	Teddy steals $50,000 from Edith's trust fund, but pays it back.
1912	➤	Teddy sells their home without Edith's knowledge.
1913	➤	Divorces Teddy.
1914	➤	Sets up American Hostels for Refugees.
1915	➤	Visits the front lines at Argonne and Verdun in France and writes about what she sees.
1916	➤	Is made Chevalier of the French Legion of Honor.
1918	➤	Receives the Medaille Reine Elisabeth (Queen Elizabeth's Medal) from Belgium for her work during the war.
1921	➤	Wins the Pulitzer Prize for *The Age of Innocence.*
1923	➤	Is the first woman to receive an honorary degree from Yale University.
1926	➤	Is elected to the National Institute of Arts and Letters.
1933	➤	*The Ladies' Home Journal* pays $25,000 for *A Backward Glance* after Edith threatens to sue them for backing out of the contract.
1937	➤	August 11, dies of a heart attack.

Learn More About Writing, and The Life And Times of Edith Wharton

- Levine, Gail Carson. *Writing Magic: Creating Stories that Fly.* Harper Collins, 2006.

- Madden, Kerry. *Writing Smarts: A Girl's Guide to Writing Great Poetry, Stories, School Reports and More!* American Girl, 2002.

- Harper, Ralph Fletcher. *How Writers Work: Finding A Process That Works For You,* Harper Trophy, 2000.

Websites:

- Short biography of Edith Wharton: http://www.kirjasto.sci.fi/wharton.htm

- Short history of 'The Gilded Age': http:/www.pbs.org/wgbh/amex.carnegie/gildedage.html

Glossary

dispensary (di SPENSS uh ree) A place where medicine or medical supplies are given out.

ear trumpet (IHR TRUHM pit) A cone-shaped instrument placed in the ear to make sounds louder.

gossip columns (GOSS ip KOL uhmz) Newspaper or magazine articles written about the rich and famous. The stories were not necessarily based on fact.

grievous (GREE vuhss) Causing suffering or sadness.

intellectual (in tuh LEK choo uhl) Involving the use of the mind.

invalids (IN vuh lidz) People who are seriously ill and often bedridden.

novella (no VE luh) Name given to a story that is between the size of a novel and a short story.

Pulitzer Prize (PUL it zuhr PRIZE) America's highest national honor for writing, named for former newspaper publisher Joseph Pulitzer.

refugee (REF yuh JEE) A person who is forced to leave his home because of war, persecution, or a natural disaster.

trust fund (TRUHST FUHND) Property or money held by one person for use by another.

— 15 —
Florence Bascom:
Geologist

by Diane Mayr

Florence Bascom had been hired at Bryn Mawr College to teach **geology**. When she got there she went to the science building. Floors one, two, and three were full. The biology, physics, and chemistry departments filled these floors. She climbed to the fourth. It was a storage area. A tiny part had been sectioned off for her office. There was no collection of rocks and minerals to teach with. She had no microscope. There wasn't even a promise of money for materials. How would she do her job?

· · · · ᏀᏅ · · · ·

Florence Bascom was born on July 14, 1862 in Williamstown, Massachusetts. Her father taught at Williams College. Both her parents believed women should be educated. They also believed in equality for women. Florence spent much time outdoors with her father. John Bascom shared his love of nature with her.

The Bascoms moved to Wisconsin when Florence was 12. Her father became president of the University of Wisconsin. Florence graduated from high school at age 15. She became a student at the university. Florence had many interests, so she studied different subjects. When she graduated she was given two **bachelor's degrees**. Most people earned only one. She decided that she liked geology. She continued studying to earn a third degree.

Women geologists were unheard of during the 1880s. Florence, though, became a geologist. She also became a **pioneer** in new field of geology. The new field was called petrography. Petrography is describing rocks and minerals in great detail. A petrographer uses a microscope to look at thin sections of rock.

Florence earned a **master's degree** at the University of Wisconsin. She wanted even more education. She went to Johns Hopkins University to work on a **doctorate degree**. In 1893 she was the first woman to earn a doctorate from the university. One newspaper reported that Florence was not at graduation. "The mention of her name, however…**evoked** round after round of applause." She missed the ceremony because she was traveling to her new job.

For two years she taught geology at Ohio State University. She next went to Bryn Mawr College in Pennsylvania. Bryn Mawr was an all-women's college. Up to that point the college had no classes in geology. Florence ended up starting the whole department. She bought, borrowed, and traded rock samples and equipment to use for teaching. She taught at Bryn Mawr for 33 years. Many of her students became respected geologists.

Florence's summers were spent doing **fieldwork**. She became the first woman appointed to the U.S. Geological Survey (USGS). The USGS made maps of the rock formations of the United States.

Florence Bascom had many "firsts" as a geologist. She was the first woman to join the Geological Society of America. She became the Society's first woman **editor**. She was its first woman officer when she became vice-president in 1930.

Florence retired from Bryn Mawr in 1932. But, she didn't stay retired. She continued her work with the USGS. She published scientific papers until 1938. In the late 1930s, Florence began to slow down. Her health became poor. She moved back to Williamstown, Massachusetts. She lived with her dogs and horses. She spent much of her time at her farmhouse, called Topping.

Florence Bascom died in 1945. She was 82 years old.

Florence Bascom, and other women on a Grand Canyon expedition in 1906.

TIDBITS

During all her years at Bryn Mawr, the geology department stayed in the 4th floor storage space.

•◆•

Bascom loved all animals, especially dogs and horses. She rode her horse, Fantasy, every day at Bryn Mawr.

•◆•

Florence not only studied rocks and minerals, she also thought they were beautiful. She had jewelry made from stones. Some of the jewelry she gave to her students.

Timeline: Florence Bascom

1862 ➤ July 14, Florence is born in Williamstown, Massachusetts, to John and Emma Curtis Bascom. She is the youngest of six children.

1874 ➤ The family moves to Madison, Wisconsin when Florence's father is named president of the University of Wisconsin. Florence enters high school and graduates in 1877.

1882–1884 ➤ Graduates from the University of Wisconsin with two bachelor degrees in arts and letters. Florence continues to study and in 1884 earns a third bachelor degree in science. She takes time off to volunteer. She teaches young black and Indian men and women at the Hampton Institute in Virginia. Florence receives no pay for this work.

1884–1887 ➤ Studies geology and petrography (rock description) at the university. Earns a master's degree in science.

1889–1893 ➤ Attends Johns Hopkins University to continue her study of petrography. Is awarded a doctorate degree in 1893 and begins teaching at Ohio State University.

1895 ➤ Is hired by Bryn Mawr College in Pennsylvania to teach geology.

1896 ➤ Becomes the first woman to work on the U.S. Geological Survey (USGS).

1896–1905 ➤ Becomes an editor for the Geological Society of America.

1907 ➤ Takes a one-year leave from teaching to study **crystallography** in Germany.

1928 ➤ Retires from teaching at Bryn Mawr. She moves to Washington, D.C. to work on USGS reports. She spends her summers at her farmhouse in Massachusetts.

1930 ➤ Is elected vice-president of the Geological Society of America.

Late 1930s ➤ Moves back to her family home in Williamstown, Massachusetts due to poor health.

1945 ➤ June 18, Florence dies in Williamstown. She is buried near her parents in the Williams College Cemetery.

Learn More About Florence Bascom and Geology

- Blobaum, Cindy. *Geology Rocks!: 50 Hands-on Activities to Explore the Earth. (Kaleidoscope Kids series.)* Ideals, 1999.

- Dixon, Dougal. *The Practical Geologist*. Simon and Schuster, 1992.

- Rice, William B. *Geologists: From Phythias to Goldring. (Mission: Science series.)* Compass Point, 2008.

- Symes, R.F. *Rocks and Minerals. (Eyewitness series.)* DK, 2004.

Websites:

- Mineralogical Society of America. "Mineralogy 4 Kids: Rockin Internet Site:" www.minsocam.org/MSA/K12/K_12.html

- U.S. Geological Survey. Robertson, Eugene C. and Kathleen Gohn. "Florence Bascom—Pioneering Geologist:" http://www.usgs.gov/125/articles/bascom.html

Glossary

bachelor's degree (BACH uh lurz di GREE) A college degree that is earned after 4 years of study.

crystallography (KRISS tuhl AW gruh fee) The study of crystals, which are clear or nearly clear minerals, like quartz.

doctorate degree (DOCK tuhr it di GREE) A college degree that is earned after receiving a master's degree.

editor (ED uh tur) Someone who checks the contents of a book, newspaper, or magazine and gets it ready to be published.

evoked (ee vohkt) Brought on.

fieldwork (FEELD wurk) Study done in nature rather than in a laboratory or a classroom.

geology (jee OL uh jee) The study of the earth's layers of soil and rock.

master's degree (MASS turz di GREE) A college degree that is earned after at least one additional year of study beyond four years of college.

pioneer (pye uh NEER) One of the first people to work in a new and unknown area.

—16—
Edith Nourse Roger:
First Massachusetts U.S. Congresswoman

by Diane Mayr

Congressman John Jacob Rogers was dead. Edith Nourse Rogers could have left Washington, D.C. Instead, she decided to run for her husband's seat in the House of Representatives. She wanted to continue his work. Edith was smart, well-traveled, and well-educated. She understood politics. The question remained--would the people of the Massachusetts Fifth District vote for a woman?

. . . . ꝏ . . . .

In 1881, Edith Nourse was born into a wealthy family in Saco, Maine. Fourteen years later, they moved to Lowell, Massachusetts. Edith's father ran a mill. Edith grew up around the mill and its workers. Her understanding of the lives of mill workers would come in handy later in her life.

Edith graduated from a private school. She went to Paris for more schooling. She then returned to Lowell. When she was 26, Edith married John Jacob Rogers.

John Jacob was a lawyer. In 1912 he ran for Congress and won. He and Edith moved to Washington, D.C. Together they worked for the people of

Massachusetts. They traveled to Europe on fact-finding trips. When World War I broke out John Jacob joined the army. Edith volunteered with the Red Cross. She nursed soldiers in France and England.

After the war, Edith continued with the Red Cross in Washington. She cared for sick and injured **veterans** at Walter Reed Army Hospital. She became known as the "Angel of Walter Reed."

In 1925, John Jacob died of cancer. Edith decided to run for her husband's seat in Congress.

The people of her district liked and respected her. They elected her on June 30, 1925.

In Congress, Edith worked to improve veterans' hospitals. She worked for **benefits** for army nurses who had served during World War I.

In the 1930s Edith realized that the Nazis in Germany were dangerous. She warned Americans about the Nazis' **persecution** of Jewish people.

War began in Europe in 1939. Edith knew that the United States would need to take part. Americans had to prepare. Women could help win the war. Although not allowed to fight, they could do other jobs. Their work would free up men for the fighting.

In 1941 Edith got busy. She thought that women should have their own branch of the Army. There were many people, though, who did not like the idea.

Then, on December 7, the Japanese attacked Pearl Harbor.

TIDBITS

Rogers often wore flowers pinned to the shoulder of her outfits. Flowers became known as her **trademark**.

• • •

Edith was quoted in the *Boston Globe* as saying that members of Congress need, "...the abilities to fight hard, fight fair, and **persevere**--all of which a woman can do as well as a man."

• • •

One of Edith's New England ancestors was Rebecca Nurse (see p. 17) who was hanged as a witch in Salem.

TIDBITS

During World War I a ship Edith traveled on was attacked by a German submarine.

◆◆

Even though she had no children of her own, Rogers was a motherly type. She was called "the mother of the WACs," "a mother to all veterans," and "the godmother of Fort Devens." (Fort Devens is a military base in Massachusetts that Edith supported.)

President Franklin Roosevelt asked Congress to declare war. By Christmas Eve, the Secretary of War backed Edith's plan. On December 31, Edith's bill was ready. The bill proposed starting a Women's Army **Auxiliary** Corps (WAAC). By May 1942, it was law.

At first, the WAACs were volunteers. Edith wanted women to receive the same benefits as men. She continued her work. The next year, the WAAC bill was replaced by one for the Women's Army Corps (WAC). Other military branches for women were soon formed.

Edith Rogers ran for Congress 18 times. As a congresswoman, she introduced more than 1,200 bills. About half had to do with veterans or the military.

In 1960, she entered a hospital in Boston with **pneumonia**. On September 10, Edith had a heart attack and died. She was 79 years old. The following Tuesday she had planned to start her 19th run for Congress. Edith Nourse Rogers probably would have won.

President Franklin Roosevelt signs Edith Nourse Rogers' bill into law. It was called "the GI Bill of Rights."

Timeline: Edith Nourse Rogers

1881 ➤ March 19 Edith is born in Saco, Maine. Her parents are Franklin Nourse and Edith Riversmith Nourse. She is educated in Lowell, Massachusetts, and Paris, France.

1907 ➤ Marries John Jacob Rogers, a lawyer. She and her husband will have no children.

1912 ➤ John Jacob Rogers is elected to the House of Representatives as a Republican. He and Edith move to Washington, D.C.

1914–1918 ➤ World War I is fought.

1917–1922 ➤ Works as a volunteer caring for disabled servicemen.

1922 ➤ President Harding appoints Edith to report on the care of disabled veterans. The next two presidents, Coolidge and Hoover, reappoint her.

1925 ➤ John Jacob dies. Edith runs as his replacement. She wins the special election and becomes the first New England woman in Congress.

1925–1960 ➤ Edith works for many causes including Massachusetts jobs, veterans' hospitals, war preparedness, military nurses. She becomes the first woman representative to sponsor a major law.

1941–1942 ➤ Legislation sponsored by Rogers leads to the start of the Women's Army Auxiliary Corps. It is replaced in 1943 by the Women's Army Corps.

1941–1945 ➤ World War II is fought. President Roosevelt sends Edith to Europe to visit military hospitals.

1944 ➤ Works for passage of the Servicemen's Readjustment Act (known as the G.I. Bill). The G.I. Bill provides educational and **financial** benefits to veterans.

1960 ➤ September 10, Edith dies in a Boston hospital. She is buried in Lowell.

Learn More about Edith Nourse Rogers, Congress, and the Causes She Supported

- Ansary, Mir Tamim. *Veterans Day, 2nd. ed. ("Holiday Histories" series).* Heinemann, 2006.

- Dubois, Muriel. *The U.S. House of Representatives ("First Facts" series).* Capstone Press, 2004

- Feldman, Ruth Tenzer. *How Congress Works: A Look at the Legislative Branch. ("How Government Works" series).* Lerner, 2004.

- Nathan, Amy. **Count on Us: American Women in the Military**. National Geographic, 2004.

Websites:

- The Dirksen Congressional Center. "Congress for Kids": http://www.congressforkids.net

- Fort Devens Museum. "Edith Nourse Rogers": http://www.fortdevensmuseum.org/EdithNourseRogers.htm

- The Office of the Clerk. "Kids in the House": http://clerkkids.house.gov

Glossary

auxiliary (awg ZIL yur ee) Helping, supporting.

benefits (BEN uh FITSS) Money paid by a government, employer, or insurance company to people for insurance, hospital care, vacation, and other things.

financial (fye NAN shuhl) Having to do with money or finances.

persecution (PUR suh kyoo shuhn) Cruel or unfair treatment of someone; abuse.

persevere (pur suh VEER) To keep trying even though there are difficulties.

pneumonia (noo MOH nyuh) A serious disease that causes the lungs to fill with liquid and makes breathing difficult.

trademark (TRADE mark) A sign or mark by which a person becomes known.

veterans (VET ur uhnz) People who have served in the armed forces especially during a war.

— 17 —
Marita Bonner:
Harlem Renaissance Writer

by M. Lu Major

Marita Bonner was born in 1898, just 35 years after slavery ended. Her own grandfather had been a slave. In many parts of the United States, the wounds of slavery still ran deep.

By the 1920s, young African American men and women were talking about change. Black artists, musicians, and writers wanted to express themselves. They did not want to imitate white art. They knew they had their own visions, music, and words. They were ready for a **rebirth** of black art. Marita was ready, too.

· · · · ᗕᎧ · · · ·

Marita grew up in Brookline, Massachusetts. Little is known about her mother but her father was a laborer. Marita's parents believed in the power of education. Marita was a good student. She wrote for her high school magazine. She became **fluent** in German and was a fine **pianist**. All three Bonner children studied hard. They received high school diplomas and went to college.

In college Marita won two music competitions. She also started the first black sorority at Radcliffe: *Delta Sigma Theta*.

◆━◆

Marita wrote three plays. The first is called *The Pot-Maker (A Play to be Read)*. People who have studied Marita's work believe all three of her plays were meant to be read rather than performed.

Marita's college life was a mixture of the bad and good that still existed in society. Black students were not allowed to live in the Radcliffe College dormitories. Marita traveled back and forth to **campus** every day.

The color of Marita's skin did not matter to her teachers. Professor Charles Copeland taught writing. Taking his class was a special honor. He only accepted 16 talented students at a time. He chose Marita. He recognized her gift with words.

After graduation, Marita taught in the south. In Washington, D.C. she met the poet Georgia Douglass Johnson. Mrs. Johnson held a weekly "salon." This gathering of talented writers helped Marita sharpen her craft.

In the early 1920s both of Marita's parents died. She feared life without her two strong anchors. Soon after their deaths she published one of her most famous essays: *On Being Young-a Woman-and Colored*. The essay explained problems faced by a young, educated, black woman in the world. It was one of the first essays to point out that women like Marita had *two* challenges. They endured prejudice as black citizens and also as women. Change would come slowly. "And you know, being a woman," Marita wrote, "you have to go about it gently and quietly to find out…just what can be done."

For twenty years Marita wrote essays, short stories, and plays. Her writing told the stories of people who had to wait "gently and quietly" while society's rules changed. They waited for equal rights. They waited for **prejudice** to die. Marita had grown up with certain privileges: education, music, and literature. Her writing, however, brought to life people who had lived in poverty. Her stories were part of the great rebirth of black art. Later, that rebirth would be called the **Harlem Renaissance**. People all over the world became part of it.

Marita married and moved to Chicago. She and her husband raised 3 children. By 1941 Marita had published her last work. She devoted the rest of her life to her family and to teaching. She taught children with special needs.

In 1971 Marita died in an apartment fire. The next year her daughter, Joyce, found some notebooks. They held six stories Marita never had published. Joyce published them in a book containing all of Marita's stories and plays.

Marita Bonner's writing was introduced to a new generation of readers.

A photo of Marita Bonner and her husband, William Occomy. Marita did not publish any more work after her marriage.

TIDBITS

In her stories, Marita invented a Chicago neighborhood called Frye Street. The people who lived on Frye Street were of different races. Marita wrote about the possibility of all people living together.

Marita's life spanned two great historical periods. She wrote during the Harlem Renaissance. She lived through the great moments of the Civil Rights Movement.

Timeline: Marita Bonner

c1898 ➤ June 15, Born in Boston to Joseph and Mary Anne Bonner. She is the third of four children.

1918 ➤ Graduates from Brookline High School.

Enters Radcliffe College.

1922 ➤ Graduates from Radcliffe College.

Moves to West Virginia and begins teaching at the Bluefield Colored Institute.

1924 ➤ Moves to Washington, D.C. and begins teaching at the Armstrong High School.

Marita's mother dies from a brain hemorrhage.

Joins the "S Street Salon" a writers' group.

1925 ➤ Publishes "The Hands—A Story" her first short story.

1926 ➤ Maritta's father dies.

December, publishes her first essay, "On Being Young-A Woman-And Colored" in NAACP's magazine: *The Crisis.*

1928 ➤ Publishes her most famous play, *The Purple Flower.*

1930s ➤ Marries William Almy Occomy.

Moves to Chicago.

They raise three children, William, Warwick, and Joyce.

No longer publishes her writing, instead, focuses on teaching students with special needs.

1941 ➤ Joins the Christian Science Church.

1963 ➤ Retires from teaching.

1971 ➤ December 6, dies from smoke inhalation as a result of an apartment fire.

c1972 ➤ Six unpublished stories are found in her notebooks but they are dated before 1941.

1987 ➤ Marita's daughter, Joyce Occomy Strickland and author Joyce Flynn publish "The Collected Works of Marita Bonner," including the unpublished stories found in Marita's notebooks.

NOTE: c1898 means about or around 1898

Learn More About Marita Bonner and the Harlem Renaissance

- Mckissack, Beringer, *Women of the Harlem Renaissance (We the People: Industrial America Series)*. Compass Point Books, 2007.
- McKissack, Patricia. *A Song for Harlem: Scraps of Time*. Viking Juvenile, 2007.
- Wallace, Maurice. *Langston Hughes: The Harlem Renaissance (Writers and Their Works)*. Benchmark Books, 2008.
- Worth, Richard. *The Harlem Renaissance: An Explosion of African-American Culture (America's Living History)*. Enslow Publishers, 2008.

Websites:

- Short profile of Marita Bonner:
  http://womenshistory.about.com/od/harlemrenaissance/p/marita_bonner.htm
- The African American Registry biography of Marita Bonner:
  http://www.aaregistry.com/african_american_history/975/Marita_Bonner_creator_of_Frye_Street

Glossary

campus (KAM puhss) The land and buildings of a college or university.

fluent (FLOO uhnt) Able to speak smoothly and clearly in another language.

Harlem Renaissance (HAR luhm REN uh sahnss) A cultural movement in 1920s America during which black art, literature, and music experienced renewal and growth, The movement began in New York City's Harlem district. Renaissance is the French word for "rebirth."

pianist (PEE uh nist) A person who plays the piano.

prejudice (PREJ uh diss) An unfair opinion about someone based on the person's race, religion, or other characteristic.

rebirth (ree BUHRTH) A revival, a new beginning.

salon (suh LAWN) An assembly of guests who gather to discuss politics, art, etc.

—18—
Katharine Lane Weems:
Sculptor

by Diane Mayr

$\mathcal{K}$atherine Lane's father took her to the studio of the famous painter, John Singer Sargent. She said, "He explained the work, showed me how he was doing it, and even asked my opinion." Her father wanted to buy her a gift as a reminder of the visit. She told him, "I saw a horse in the studio whose skin was peeled off so you could study his muscles. Do you think you could get me one like that?" Many people would have thought that her request was strange, but not her father. He found a model horse for her.

· · · · ⚬ · · · ·

Katherine Ward Lane was born on February 22, 1899. Her family and friends called her Kay. Her father worked in **finance**. Her mother did what was expected of rich women--she **socialized** and did **volunteer** work. She thought Kay would grow up and do the same.

Kay, an only child, spent a lot of time with her father. He often took her to the Boston Museum of Fine Arts (MFA). Sadly, he died shortly after their visit to John Singer Sargent's studio in 1914.

Kay's mother thought she should attend the Museum School at the MFA. It would take her mind off her father's death. At first Kay took drawing classes. She found that she liked clay **modeling**. Charles Grafly, a famous sculptor, taught at the Museum School. Kay's early attempts were not good. With Grafly's help she improved.

Kay became good friends with sculptor Anna Vaughn Hyatt. Hyatt taught Kay the importance of looking at live animals to see how the muscles and other parts of the body moved. Kay studied in Anna Hyatt's New York City studio. Another artist, Brenda Putnam, taught Kay **anatomy** and drawing. Kay understood that "an animal is forever in movement." She wanted to show motion in her work. She spent many hours at the Bronx Zoo studying, drawing, and sculpting animals.

Not only did she keep busy with her art, Kay also kept a busy social schedule. She had many friends. Several men asked her to marry them, but she turned them down. For Kay, art was more important than marriage.

Kay began to show her work in the early 1920s. She started winning awards. In 1930, Kay was filmed with her greyhound, Dark Warrior. The movie, *From Clay to **Bronze*** shows how a bronze sculpture is made from start to finish.

Harvard University built a new **biology** building. They

TIDBITS

Kay was named after her aunt Katharine Ward Lane. Her aunt was a watercolor painter who died 6 years before Kay was born.

◆

Kay started keeping a diary when she was in her teens. Her 1985 book *Odds Were Against Me* was written from the diaries she kept between 1914 and 1966.

TIDBITS

Kay was an animalier. An animalier is an artist who sculpts or paints animals.

◆•◆

Kay often found it hard to believe in herself. When she won her first gold medal, she wrote, "It can't have been a very good exhibition this year if I got the prize."

◆•◆

Kay made small sculptures of her dog, Yvonne. The sculptures were made into **hood ornaments** for cars.

hired Kay to decorate the front of the building. She designed large **friezes** that were 400 feet long. She created bronze doors. She sculpted two life-sized rhinoceroses for the front of the building. The project took seven years to finish.

Kay's longtime friend, F. Carrington Weems, asked her to marry him in 1947. She decided the time was right. But, as she had thought when she was younger, marriage took her away from her art. For many years afterward she only drew. She didn't work on large sculptures until after her husband's death in 1966.

In the 1970s, Kay grew interested in dolphins. She sculpted a 12' long group of six dolphins swimming together. She lived for ten more years after she finished it in 1979. *Dolphins of the Sea* is seen each year by thousands of people in front of the New England Aquarium.

Dolphins of the Sea *by Katharine Lane Weems*

Timeline: Katharine Lane Weems

1899 ➤ February 22, is born in Boston, Massachusetts to Gardiner Martin Lane and Emma Louise Gildersleeve Lane.

1914 ➤ Travels to Europe with her parents. Visits the studio of artist, John Singer Sargent.

October, Kay's father dies.

1918 ➤ Meets the sculptor, Anna Vaughn Hyatt (later known as Anna Hyatt Huntington). Begins taking classes at the Museum of Fine Arts. She is the student of sculptor Charles Grafly.

1921 ➤ Takes private lessons from Anna Hyatt in New York. Spends time at the Bronx Zoo where she studies the animals.

1924–1927 ➤ Begins exhibiting her animal bronzes and wins several awards including the George D. Widener Memorial Gold Medal for *Narcisse Noir*, a sculpture of a dog.

1930 ➤ Stars in a short film, *From Clay to Bronze*.

1930–1937 ➤ Works on the Biological Laboratories building at Harvard University.

1941–1945 ➤ During World War II, volunteers for the Red Cross and gives speeches to help raise money. Creates the Medal of Merit for the U.S. government.

1947 ➤ November 15, marries F. Carrington Weems, and moves to New York City.

1952 ➤ Is elected to National Institute of Arts and Letters.

1965 ➤ In memory of her mother, who died in 1954, Katharine donates 40 of her sculptures to the Boston Museum of Science.

1966 ➤ Husband, Carrington Weems, dies after seven years of illness.

1974 ➤ Begins work on *Dolphins of the Sea* for the New England Aquarium. It is finished in 1979.

1985 ➤ Publishes her book *Odds Were Against Me: A Memoir*. Her final exhibit is held in Boston.

1989 ➤ February 11, dies in Boston.

Learn More About Katherine Lane Weems and Sculpting

- Muybridge, Eadweard. *Animals in Motion*. Dover, 1957.
- Nardo, Don. *Sculpture. ("Eye on Art" series)*. Gale, 2006.
- Temple, Kathryn. *Art for Kids: Drawing: The Only Drawing Book You'll Ever Need to Be the Artist You've Always Wanted to Be.* Lark Books, 2005.

Websites:

- Boyce, Michael. "The Bronze Process." A short video showing how bronze sculptures are made:
  http://michaelboyce.net/video.php
- Harvey, Andre. "Bronze Sculpture: Lost Wax Process." Explains and illustrates the steps in taking a clay sculpture and making it into a bronze sculpture:
  http://www.andreharvey.com/wax.html
- Museum of Science, Boston. "Weems Animal Sculptures Audio Slideshow:"
  http://www.mos.org/events_activities/lyman_library&d = 1819
- Riedel, Catherine. "Antiques: Creatures in Bronze: Katherine Lane Weems Loved to Sculpt Animals:"
  http://www.yankeemagazine.com/issues/2008-03/home/sculpting

Glossary

anatomy (uh NAT uh mee) The scientific study of the structure of plants or animals.

biology (bye OL uh jee) The scientific study of living things.

bronze (BRONZ) A hard, reddish brown metal that is a mixture of copper and tin.

finance (FYE nanss) The management of money and investments.

friezes (FREEZ uhz) Bands, usually on the upper part of outside walls, that are decorated with sculpture or lettering.

hood ornaments (HOOD OR nuh muhntss) Small metal sculptures that are attached to the hood of a car as decorations.

modeling (MOD uh ling) Making a copy or representation of something, usually in clay.

socialized (SOH shuh lized) Took part in activities with other rich people.

volunteer (VOL uhn TIHR) To work without pay.

—19—
Bette Davis:
Actress

by Barbara J. Turner

"*L*earn the lead part, Bette."

Bette wondered what Mother meant. She had the smallest part in the play, not the lead. Still, Mother always gave good advice. So, as the train chugged toward Rochester, NY, Bette studied her lines and those of the lead actress.

Two days after the play opened, the lead actress fell down a flight of stairs. It was part of the play. But she wasn't supposed to sprain her ankle. When she did, a new lead had to be found.

Bette knew the lines. She got the part.

· · · · ౧౦ · · · ·

Ruth Elizabeth Davis was born April 5, 1908, in Lowell, Massachusetts. Her parents called her Bette. When she was seven, her parents separated.

Bette originally spelled her name B-E-T-T-Y. When she was 17, a neighbor suggested she change it to B-E-T-T-E to be different. Bette liked being different and standing out. She changed the spelling of her name.

•—•—

Bette believed in being prepared for opportunities. She said, "Even the opportunity to fail is worth something, especially if you get another opportunity to succeed . . . ."

Times were hard, but Bette's mother gave her everything she could. When Bette said she wanted to be an actress, her mother whisked her off to one of the best acting schools in New York, promising to pay the owner later.

Bette studied hard. She learned to walk, talk and fall. She learned to memorize lines. One day, a talent scout saw her in a play. He asked her to come to Hollywood. She took a **screen test** for Univeral **Studios**. They didn't think Bette looked right for the part. Instead, as part of her **contract,** Universal **loaned** her out to other studios.

When her contract expired, Bette prepared to go home. As she packed, the phone rang. It was George Arliss from Warner Brothers. He had seen Bette in a movie. She would be perfect for the lead in his new film. Was she interested?

Yes! Bette signed the contract and began making movies, but she could not choose her own roles. At that time, studios made all the decisions for their actors. Bette wanted to make her own choices. She refused to make any more movies unless she could choose some roles herself. Warner Brothers **suspended** her without pay.

Bette did not take this lying down. She sued them. Warner Brothers was stunned. Some actors complained about their contracts. Some, like Bette, refused to work. But to be sued? By a woman? It was unheard of!

Bette flew to England to make two movies there. Warner Brothers served her with an **injunction.** It forbade her to act for anyone else until their case was settled. They went to court and

Bette lost. Her contract might be unfair, but she had signed it.

Still, Bette gained the respect of Warner Brothers. They paid her court costs, gave her better parts and increased her **salary.** Her **lawsuit** also gave courage to other actors. Olivia de Haviland sued Warner Brothers a few years later and won her case. Now actors had more control of their own careers. Bette had paved the way.

Bette made many more movies. She won two Best Actress Oscars, and was the first woman elected President of the Academy of Motion Picture Arts and Sciences. She was also the first woman to receive the American Film Institute's Lifetime Achievement award. In 1987, after battling breast cancer, a stroke, and a broken hip, she made *The Whales of August* at age 79. She died two years later in France.

Bette said, "One thing I'm proud of, I can tell you, is that I always gave my best."

Bette Davis and actor Spencer Tracy with their Oscars in 1938.

Timeline: Bette Davis

1908	➤ April 5, Ruth Elizabeth Davis is born in Lowell, Massachusetts to Ruth Favor and Harlow Morrell Davis.
1927	➤ She is accepted at the John Murray Anderson School of Theater and Dance.
1930	➤ Arrives at Universal Studios and makes her first film, *Bad Sister*.
1931	➤ Signs with Warner Brothers.
1932	➤ August 18, marries Harmon 'Ham' O. Nelson.
1935	➤ Wins the Best Actress Academy Award for *Dangerous*.
1936	➤ Sues Warner Brothers to get out of her contract and loses.
1938	➤ Wins the Best Actress Academy Award for *Jezebel*.
1940	➤ December 31, marries second husband Arthur Austin Farnsworth.
1941	➤ Is elected the first female President of the Motion Picture Academy. Joins "Stars Over America," and sells war bonds.
1942	➤ Opens the Hollywood Canteen with John Garfield.
1945	➤ November 30, marries third husband, William Grant Sherry.
1947	➤ May 1, gives birth to daughter, Barbara Davis Sherry.
1948	➤ Demands to be let out of her contract and quits Warner Brothers.
1950	➤ July 28, marries fourth husband Gary Merrill.
1957	➤ Breaks her back in a fall down a flight of stairs.
1962	➤ Makes a comeback in *Whatever Happened to Baby Jane?*
1977	➤ Receives the American Film Institute's Lifetime Achievement Award.
1980	➤ Wins an Emmy for *Strangers*.
1983	➤ Diagnosed with breast cancer. Has a stroke nine days later.
1987	➤ Receives Kennedy Center Honors.
1988	➤ Writes *This 'N That* with Michael Herskowitz.
1989	➤ October 6, dies in France at age 81.
2008	➤ U.S. Post Office honors Bette Davis with a stamp.

Learn More About Bette Davis and Being an Actor:

- Bany-Winters, Lisa. *Showtime: Music, Dance and Drama Activities for Kids.* Chicago Review Press, 2005.

- Friedman, Lise and Dowdle, Mary. *Break a Leg! The Kids' Guide to Acting and Stagecraft.* Workman Publishing Company, 2002.

- Peterson, Lenka and O'Connor, Dan. *Kids Take the Stage: Helping Young People Discover The Creative Outlet of Theater.* Backstage Books, 2nd revised edition, 2006.

Websites:

- The official Bette Davis website: http://www.bettedavis.com

- Theater Games: http://library.thinkquest.org/5291/games.html

Glossary

contract (KON trakt) A legal agreement between people or companies that states the terms by which one will work for the other.

injunction (in JUHNK shuhn) A written order from a court to do or stop doing something.

lawsuit (LAW soot) A legal action or case brought against a person or a group in a court of law.

loaned (LOHND) Lending something; when movie studios allowed actors to work for other studios the actor was said to be "loaned" to the other studio.

salary (SAL uh ree) A fixed amount of money someone is paid to work.

screen test (SKREEN TEST) A short film made to check whether an actor should be used for a particular role in a movie.

studios (STOO dee ohz) Places where movies, TV and radio shows, or CD recordings are made.

sued (SOOD) Taking a case against someone to court.

suspended (suh SPEND ed) Stopping something (like work) for a short time.

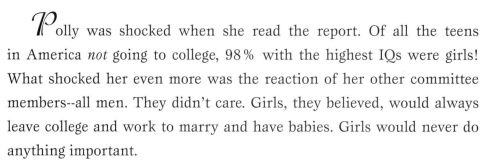

—20—
Mary 'Polly' Ingraham Bunting:
Scientist and Reformer

by Barbara J. Turner

*P*olly was shocked when she read the report. Of all the teens in America *not* going to college, 98% with the highest IQs were girls! What shocked her even more was the reaction of her other committee members--all men. They didn't care. Girls, they believed, would always leave college and work to marry and have babies. Girls would never do anything important.

Polly could not believe it. She made up her mind to prove them wrong.

· · · · ⌒ · · · ·

Mary Ingraham was born in Brooklyn, New York on July 10, 1910. Everyone called her Polly, the English nickname for Mary. Polly was curious about everything. She banded birds. She kept bees. She slept outside--even in winter--to study the stars. In 1927, her curiosity took her to college, where she studied **bacteria.**

Polly was curious about what bacteria did. She set up **experiments** and learned how bacteria grew and changed. Soon, she became an expert and published several important papers. In 1934, she received her **Ph.D.** and took a teaching position at Bennington College in Vermont where she taught for two years.

In 1937, Polly married Henry Bunting. She followed him to Yale University where he did his **residency** in **pathology**. She got a job there doing research. In 1940, she had her first child, Mary. Like most women, she gave up her career for her family. When Henry died in 1954, Polly had four children and needed to support them. A friend offered her a job as Dean of Douglas College, an all-girl school.

At Douglas, Polly saw many girls leave school after they married. She wondered why. She found women were not allowed to attend college part-time. If they had children, they were discouraged from coming back. Then she attended the meeting where she learned women were not expected to do anything important.

Polly knew many women *did* want careers, so why didn't they **pursue** them? She studied the problem and saw that a man's path differed from a woman's. A married man could go from college to work without interruption. Women couldn't. They had children, husbands, and homes to care for. They needed a different path. Polly found one for them. She convinced Douglas College to accept married women as part-time students.

Radcliffe, another all-girl college, heard about Polly. They asked her to work for them. Polly went to Radcliffe with an idea. Radcliffe could give money to married women. These **fellowships** would let women hire babysitters and have time to study.

TIDBITS

When studying for exams, Polly would stand on her head to clear it. She said it gave her a different perspective.

•◆•

Until 1940, no one knew where chimney swifts went in winter time. Then two were found in the jungles of South America. They were chimney swifts Polly had banded.

•◆•

Polly moved many times in her life and always took her bees with her. At Radcliffe, she set her bee hives up on the college roof.

But being President of the college did not mean Polly could do what she wanted. She needed permission from the **board of trustees.** The board did not like Polly's idea. They felt there was no money for such a program.

Polly asked her friends for help. She asked wealthy Americans for **donations**. Soon, everyone knew about Polly's project. The *New York Times* wrote a front page story about it. *TIME Magazine* put her on their cover. America buzzed with her 'theory of unexpectation" --the belief that girls did not achieve because no one expected them to.

Finally, in 1961, the Radcliffe Institute for Independent Study opened its doors to twenty women. The Institute grew and grew, and in 1978, it was renamed the Mary Ingraham Bunting Institute in Polly's honor. It still exists today.

Polly retired from Radcliffe in 1972, but her work there encouraged other women's colleges to make changes, too. Polly's work gave women the chance to have it all - a family, an education, *and* a career.

Polly Bunting always enjoyed being outdoors. Here, she canoes with two of her children

Timeline: Mary 'Polly' Ingraham Bunting:

1910 ➤ July 10, Mary Ingraham is born in Brooklyn, New York to Henry A. and Mary Shotwell Ingraham.

1927–1931 ➤ Attends Vassar College.

1931 ➤ Attends graduate school at the University of Wisconsin.

1933 ➤ Publishes her first paper on bacteria in the *Journal of Bacteriology*.

1934 ➤ Receives her PhD two and a half years early.

1935 ➤ Teaches Physiology and Genetics at Bennington College in Vermont.

1937 ➤ June 22, marries Henry Bunting.

1940–1947 ➤ Polly and Henry have 4 children: Mary, Charles, William, and John.

1946 ➤ Teaches bacteriology at Wellesley College.

1954 ➤ April 15, Henry Bunting dies of a malignant brain tumor.

1955 ➤ Polly is appointed Dean of Douglas College.

1959 ➤ Convinces Douglas College to accept ten married women as part time students.

Leaves Douglas College and becomes President of Radcliffe.

1961 ➤ Begins a new program, The Radcliffe Institute for Independent Studies.

1964 ➤ Is appointed the first female **commissioner** of the Atomic Energy Commission.

1972 ➤ Becomes Assistant to the President for Special Projects at Princeton University.

1975 ➤ Retires from Princeton and moves to her farm house in New Boston, NH.

1978 ➤ The Radcliffe Institute for Independent Studies is renamed The Mary Ingraham Bunting Institute.

1979 ➤ May 19, marries Clem Smith.

1991 ➤ Clem dies. Polly moves into a retirement community in Hanover, NH.

1992 ➤ Sells her New Boston property and gives her marsh lands to the town.

1998 ➤ January 21, Polly dies.

1999 ➤ Radcliffe merges with Harvard University. The Mary Ingraham Bunting Institute is renamed The Radcliffe Institute Fellowship Program at the Radcliffe Institute for Advanced Study at Harvard University.

Learn More About "Polly" Bunting and Women Scientists and Activists

- Lassieur, Allison. *Eleanor Roosevelt: Activist for Change.* Franklin Watts, 2007.
- Stile, Darlene R. *Extraordinary Women Scientists.* Children's Press, 2005.
- Yaffe, Elaine. *Mary Ingraham Bunting: Her Two Lives!* Frederic C. Beil, 2005.

Websites:

- Science experiences for girls across the country:
  http://pbskids.org/dragonflytv/gps/scigirls.html

Glossary

bacteria (bak TIHR ee uh) Microscopic living things that exist in and around you. Some are useful but some cause disease.

board of trustees (bord uhv truhss TEEZ) A group of people who that run an organization or business.

commissioner (kuh MISH uhn ur) A person who is in charge of certain tasks or is elected to solve a particular problem.

donations (doh NAY shunz) Money given for a cause.

experiments (ek SPER uh mentss) Scientific tests to try out a theory.

fellowships (FEL oh shipss) Money given to a special student (called a "fellow") for study at a college or university.

pathology (path AW luh gee) The study of disease.

PhD (pee aych DEE) An abbreviation for Doctor of Philosophy. A PhD is the highest degree a student may receive at a university. Those who that receive this degree are called "Doctor" to show that they are experts in their fields of study.

pursue (pur SOO) To go after; to chase.

residency (REZ uh duhn see) Advanced training in a medical specialty.

—21—
Nancy Harkness Love:
First Woman to Fly for the Military

by Janet Buell

Sixteen-year old Nancy Harkness peered out the open cockpit. Below, the earth looked green, gray and vast. The airplane zipped through clouds Nancy had only seen from the ground. "What do you think?" the pilot shouted. "Great!" she yelled back. Rushing air ripped the word away.

Nancy knew then she had to keep flying.

· · · · ◯ · · · ·

Nancy Harkness was born on Valentine's Day in 1914. Eleven years earlier, the Wright brothers flew the first airplane. Few women piloted airplanes in the early days of flying. Most women didn't even drive cars.

Nancy's parents paid for her flying lessons. In a month she had received her pilot's license. The sixteen year old was now the youngest female pilot in the US.

When she went to college, Nancy rented planes from a nearby airfield. College kids paid her to give them rides. She also gave flying lessons. Nancy quit college after two years to sell airplanes in Boston.

The Bureau of Air **Commerce** hired Nancy to be part of their air-marking program. She was only 21 years old. Nancy flew from New

England to Florida. She looked for rooftops, water towers, and landmarks visible from the air. These would then be painted with town names and compass headings. The markings helped guide other pilots flying overhead.

In 1936, Nancy married fellow pilot Robert Love. Headlines trumpeted the wedding. "BEAUTIFUL **AVIATRIX** WEDS DASHING AIR CORPS OFFICER." The Loves took off on a flying honeymoon. Later, they ran their Boston-based company, Inter City Aviation.

In 1942, Japan air-bombed the U.S. military base at Pearl Harbor. The surprise attack pulled the U.S. into the World War II. Robert was called for military duty in Washington, D.C. Nancy got a job in Baltimore. She flew herself to work every day.

Colonel William Tunner heard about the young flier. Tunner commanded the Air Transport division of the army. US factories made airplanes to support our troops in Europe. Every able-bodied man went to war overseas. Tunner needed more pilots to fly planes to military bases.

Tunner didn't know much about women fliers. He wasn't sure they could do the job. Still, he needed **ferry pilots**. He asked Nancy to write down her ideas.

Tunner liked Nancy's ideas. He chose her to command a new air group called the Women's **Auxiliary** Ferrying **Squadron** (WAFS).

Nancy found twenty-five expert pilots. The women went through tough military training. The training and requirements were tougher than the men's. Eventually, 404 women became

WAFS pilots. The women flew 12,000 airplanes a month. Women fliers freed up 1,704 male fighter pilots.

The job was dangerous. Thirty-eight WAFS lost their lives in airplane crashes. The U.S. government paid death benefits when a male pilot died. When a female pilot died, the government paid nothing. The woman's family paid to ship her body back home.

The WAFS merged with another women's flying group in 1943. They became WASP (Women's Air Force Service Pilots). Nancy kept command of the ferrying division.

World War II was winding down in 1944. The government **disbanded** the WASP. No newspapers covered the story. The WASP quietly disappeared to private life. Many still continued to fly.

Nancy went home to raise a family. She kept working to get the WASP military benefits. In 1977, the US formally recognized WASP as military. Nancy didn't live to see this happen. She died in 1976.

Three WASP prepare for a flight.

TIDBITS

Nancy demanded that her pilots always behave properly. One mistake could turn public feelings against the women fliers.

Male pilots didn't like the P-39 high-speed fighter plane. They called it the "flying coffin." Tunner believed the men weren't flying the plane according to directions. He had the women fly it. They had no trouble at all. After that, the men no longer complained about the airplane.

Timeline: Nancy Harkness Love

1914 ➤ February 14, Nancy Harkness is born in Houghton, Michigan to Robert and Alice Graham Harkness on February 14, 1914.

1927 ➤ Nancy travels and studies throughout Europe. She witnesses Charles Lindbergh's historic landing in France.

1930 ➤ November 7, receives her private pilot's license.

1931 ➤ Enters Vassar College. She is the only female flier at the college.

1933 ➤ Earns her transport license.

1934 ➤ Drops out of Vassar with "the strange idea that I could get a job in aviation," as she would later write. Takes a job as a **demo** pilot and sales person.

1935–1937 ➤ Joins the Bureau of Air Commerce's air-marking program. Helps place 290 markers in Massachusetts.

1936 ➤ January 11, marries Robert Love.

1937–1938 ➤ Test pilot for the Gwinn Aircar Company. Tests the first tricycle landing gear.

1940 ➤ May 20, sends a letter to Colonel Robert Olds. In it, she lists 104 women who should be considered for an air ferrying program.

1942 ➤ Nancy becomes commander of WAFS and recruits 25 experienced female pilots, known as "The Originals."

1943 ➤ June, Nancy selected as commander of four WAF squadrons.

August 5, WAFS merge with the Women's Flying Training Detachment and become the WASP.

1944 ➤ December 20, the WASP are disbanded.

1947 ➤ Daughter Hannah born.

1949 ➤ Daughter Margaret born.

1951 ➤ Daughter Alice born.

1976 ➤ October 22, Nancy dies of cancer.

1977 ➤ November 23, Congress officially gives WASP official military recognition. WASP can now collect the same benefits as male **veterans.**

Learn More About Nancy Harkness Love and Women Pilots:

- Atkins, Jeannine. *Wings and Rockets: The Story of Women in Air and Space.* Farrar, Straus, and Giroux, 2003.

- Donelly, Karen. *American Women Pilots of World War II*. Rosen Publishing, 2004.

- Holden, Henry M. *American Women of Flight: Pilots and Pioneers.* Enslow Publishing, 2003.

- Nathan, Amy. *Yankee Doodle Gals: Women Pilots of World War II*. National Geographic Children's Books, 2001.

Websites:

- The American Experience: Nancy Harkness Love: http://www.pbs.org/wgbh/amex/flygirls/peopleevents/pandeamex03.html

- WASP on the Web: read, learn, play games: http://www.wingsacrossamerica.us/wasp/

Glossary

auxiliary (awg ZIL yur ee) A group that gives help or extra support.

aviatrix (AY vee AY trikss) A woman pilot.

buzzed (BUHZD) Flew low and close to a building, trees, or people.

commerce (KOM urss) The buying and selling of things in order to make money.

demo (DEM oh) Short for "demonstration." A sample.

disbanded (diss BAND uhd) The word used when an organization has been taken apart.

ferry pilot (FER ee PYE luht) A person who flies planes from the place where they were manufactured to the airbase where they will be used.

squadron (SKWAHD ruhn) A group of ships, cavalry troops, or other military units.

veterans (VET urh uhnz) Someone who has served in the Armed Forces.

—22—
Joyce Chen:
Chef

by Diane Mayr

*I*t is Thanksgiving, 1981. Joyce Chen will be cooking for her family—and 40 guests. She knows how hard it is for students from China to be far from their homes and families. She knows they miss "real" home cooking. Joyce Chen also knows that American holidays and foods are sometimes a mystery to them. Joyce will share her cooking and what she has learned about America. The students will eat dumplings and roast turkey. They will learn a little about America and a lot about the kindness of Joyce Chen.

· · · · ᧓ · · · ·

Liao Jia-ai was born in China in 1917. Her family was rich and had servants. Jia-ai and her mother did not need to cook or do housework. Her mother told her, "You never know what the future will bring, and you don't want to eat raw rice." So, Jia-ai learned to cook by watching and doing. As an adult she remembered making child-size pastries alongside the family chef.

112

At the time, it was popular for people in China to take an English name. Jia-ai's teacher chose the name "Joyce" for her. The teacher thought Jia-ai always seemed happy and joyful in class.

Joyce cooked her first party **banquet** at age 18. She continued to cook and learn all she could. In her mid-twenties, Joyce married Chen Da-zhong. His English name was Thomas Chen.

Then, in April 1949, life changed. People known as **Communists** took over the government of China. Not everyone in China was happy with the new government. Many left the country. The Communists tried to stop people from entering or leaving. The Chen family fled on the last boat out of Shanghai.

They settled in Cambridge, Massachusetts where they had friends. The Chens often invited Chinese students to their home. Joyce's Chinese cooking was a treat. "I made them feel at home," she said. "And they made me feel the same in this new country."

Joyce's daughter, Helen, took cookies and eggrolls to a school bake sale. Helen told her mother she hadn't seen the eggrolls being sold. Joyce was afraid they weren't good and hadn't been put out. She later met one of the mothers in charge of the sale table. The woman told her that the eggrolls sold in 5 minutes. Joyce was surprised and pleased. Not only Chinese, but also Americans, liked her cooking!

Chinese restaurants in America served dishes such as chop suey. Chop suey was not an **authentic** dish. Joyce wanted people

TIDBITS

In China, last names are written first. Liao is the family, or last name. Jia-ai is the given name. When she took the first name of Joyce, her full name, written in the English way, was Joyce Liao.

◆

"Cooking is an art—an unselfish art which you will enjoy sharing with others." from the *Joyce Chen Cook Book*.

113

TIDBITS

Joyce Chen is remembered as the "godmother of Chinese cooking." She cooked in the Mandarin style of the northern region of China.

•◆•

She enjoyed all kinds of food and cooking. Her son, Stephen said, "People don't know this, but her best dish was Russian borscht." Borscht is a type of beet soup.

•◆•

Children who visited her restaurant were given a Tootsie Pop as they left.

to eat the real thing. So, in May 1958 she opened the Joyce Chen Restaurant. She served authentic and healthy Chinese food.

Her American friends were curious about Chinese cooking. Was it hard to do? She started to teach classes. Then, in 1962, she published the *Joyce Chen Cook Book*. It had color photos so that cooks could see the way the dishes should look when finished.

Joyce became the first Chinese American to **host** a regular television program. "Joyce Chen Cooks" was seen nationwide on public television. She also started a business to sell Chinese **cookware**.

When she was in her 60s Joyce Chen developed an illness called **Alzheimer's Disease**. It slowly weakened her body and her mind. She had to retire from business. Joyce Chen died in August 1994.

Today, her children carry on her work of making Chinese cooking a part of American life.

Joyce Chen cooking

114

Timeline: Joyce Chen

1917	➤	September 14, Liao Jia-ai is born in Peking (now called Beijing), China. She is the only child of her father's second wife, but she has 8 step-siblings. When she is in her teens, the family moves to Shanghai.
c1942	➤	Marries Chen Da-zhong (English name Thomas Chen).
1944	➤	Son, Henry, is born.
1946	➤	Daughter, Helen, is born.
1949	➤	April, the Chen family flees when the Communists take over in China. They settle in Cambridge, MA.
1952	➤	Son Stephen is born.
1958	➤	Opens the Joyce Chen restaurant.
1960	➤	Begins teaching adult education classes in Chinese cooking.
1962	➤	Publishes the *Joyce Chen Cook Book*.
1966	➤	Joyce and husband, Thomas, divorce.
1968	➤	"Joyce Chen Cooks" begins on public television. Shares a **studio** kitchen with the French Chef, Julia Child. Julia Child is 6' 2" tall. Joyce has to wear high heels so that she can reach the counter tops!
1972	➤	Travels back to China with her children. The visit is filmed. "Joyce Chen's China" is shown on public television.
1985	➤	Is diagnosed with Alzheimer's disease.
1994	➤	August 23, Joyce Chen dies in Lexington, MA at the age of 76. Her children continue in the business of Chinese cooking. They run her restaurant until it closes in 1998, write cookbooks, or sell Chinese cooking utensils and "Joyce Chen" products such as Peking Ravioli.

NOTE: c1942 means about or around 1942

Learn More About Joyce Chen, Chinese Americans, and Chinese Cooking

- Anderson, Dale. *Chinese Americans. ("American Immigrants" series)*. Rourke, 2008.
- Burckhardt, Ann L. *People of China and Their Food. ("Multicultural Cookbooks" series)*. Capstone, 1996.
- Martin, Michael. *Chinese Americans. ("Immigrants in America" series)*. Chelsea House, 2003.
- Simonds, Nina, Lesley Schwartz, and the Children's Museum, Boston. *Moonbeams, Dumplings & Dragon Boats: A Treasury of Chinese Holiday Tales, Activities & Recipes*. Harcourt, 2002.

Websites:

- See your name translated into Chinese characters: http://www.chinesenames.org/
- Asia Education Foundation. "Lesson Plan: Student Sheet 2: Using Chopsticks" http://www.asiaeducation.edu.au/china/virtual/lesson/chop2.htm

Glossary

Alzheimer's Disease (AWLTS hye muhrz duh ZEEZ) A disease of the nervous system that damages brain cells. People who develop Alzheimer's disease slowly lose their memory.

authentic (aw THEN tik) Real or genuine.

banquet (BANG kwit) A formal meal for a large number of people, usually on a special occasion.

Communists (KOM yuh nistss) People who follow a form of government where all property, including one's home and business, is supposed to be shared.

cookware (KUK wair) Pots, utensils, and other equipment used in cooking.

host (HOHST) The person who is in charge of what goes on during a television program.

studio (STOO dee oh) A place where radio or television programs are recorded or filmed.

Eunice Kennedy Shriver:

Founder of the Special Olympics

by Andrea Murphy

Eunice cut an article from the newspaper. She wanted her children to know what was happening in the world. The article told about children starving in **Biafra**. Eunice knew she had to help.

She put the article on the table next to a piggy bank. She stuffed thirty dollars into the bank. That's what the Shriver's dinner would have cost. Thirty dollars would feed lots of starving children.

That night the Shrivers ate cereal.

· · · · ⟡ · · · ·

Eunice Mary Kennedy was born in Brookline, Massachusetts on July 10, 1921. Her father, Joe, was a successful businessman. Her mother, Rose, came from an important Boston family.

Eunice adored her parents. Joe taught her to love **competition**. He taught her the importance of **politics**. Rose taught Eunice that all people mattered. No one should be left behind or left out. Eunice's deep religious faith came from her mother. So did her love of family.

TIDBITS

"Mental retardation" describes people who learn more slowly than other people their own age. In 2004, the Special Olympics began using the term "intellectual disabilities" instead of "mental retardation."

◆—◆

After college, Eunice wanted to help people in need. She became a social worker. She worked with women prisoners in West Virginia. She worked with **juvenile delinquents** in Chicago.

Eunice grew up smack in the middle of nine brothers and sisters – Joseph, John, Rosemary, Kathleen, Eunice, Patricia, Robert, Jean and Ted. Eunice loved them with all her heart. She especially loved her big sister, Rosemary. Rosemary was a person with **intellectual disability**, often called I.D. It was harder for her to learn things.

As Eunice got older, she watched out for Rosemary. Eunice's brother Ted said, "Eunice would spend the extra time with Rosemary. Teaching her and making sure that she felt included."

In 1953, Eunice married Robert Sargent Shriver, Jr. They would have five children, but that would not stop her from helping people.

Her brother, John, became a congressman. Later, he became a senator. Eunice told him he should help people in need. She knew politics could get good things done.

John became president of the United States in 1960. Eunice urged him to help people with I.D. The President Kennedy Committee on Mental Retardation was formed in 1961. Eunice worked with the committee to make life better for people with I.D. Still, she knew she could do more.

Eunice started a summer day camp at her home in 1962. People with I.D. came to Camp Shriver. They participated in sports and physical activities. The campers loved it.

Eunice got people to help. Friends gave money and volunteered at the camp. Her children worked at the camp. It still wasn't enough. She knew she could do more.

In 1968, Eunice organized the first Special Olympic Games in Chicago. That summer, around 1,000 athletes competed in **aquatics**, floor hockey and other athletics.

Today, summer and winter Special Olympic Games are held around the world. Over one million athletes from 160 countries participate. They compete in 26 sports. Eunice had a special **mission** in life. She wanted to make the world safe for people with I.D. She also wanted people to know that everyone has something to give. Even people with I.D.

A **tribute** to Eunice was held at the John F. Kennedy Presidential Library and Museum on November 16, 2007. Her brother, Senator Ted Kennedy spoke. "In our family, we were all taught that we could make a difference and all of us should try," said Ted. "And what a difference Eunice has made!"

TIDBITS

During World War II, her brother Joe was killed. Shortly after, her sister Kathleen died. Her brothers, President John Kennedy and Senator Robert Kennedy, were both shot and killed. Eunice's faith helped her carry on.

•◆•

"I love to be with my special friends and I like to learn from them. I learn persistence. I learn guts. I learn courage," Eunice said, speaking about people with I.D. at the JFK Presidential Library Tribute to her.

Today, more than a million Special Olympians compete in 26 sports.

Timeline: Eunice Kennedy Shriver

1921	➤	July 10, Eunice Mary is born the fifth of nine children to Joseph and Rose Kennedy in Brookline, Massachusetts.
1938	➤	Eunice's father is appointed Ambassador to Britain. The whole family moves to London.
1944	➤	Eunice graduates from Stanford University with a degree in sociology.
1950	➤	Eunice becomes a social worker at the Penitentiary for Women in Alderson, West Virginia.
1951	➤	Eunice moves to Chicago, Illinois to work with the House of the Good Shepherd and the Chicago Juvenile Court.
1953	➤	May 23, Eunice marries Robert Sargent Shriver, Jr. They would have five children – Bobby, Maria, Timothy, Mark, and Anthony.
1957	➤	Becomes director of the Joseph P. Kennedy, Jr. Foundation.
1962	➤	June, Camp Shriver, a summer day camp for children and adults with I.D., opens at Timberlawn, Shriver's home in Rockville, Maryland.
1968	➤	July 20, the First International Special Olympics Summer Games is held in Chicago, Illinois.
1982	➤	Founds Community of Caring, a character education program in over 1,200 schools.
1984	➤	March 14, receives The Presidential Medal of Freedom from President Ronald Reagan.
1995	➤	Eunice is pictured on the 1995 **commemorative** Special Olympics World Games Silver Dollar. She is the only living woman ever to be featured on a United States coin.
1998	➤	Eunice is inducted into the National Women's Hall of Fame.
2002	➤	Eunice receives the Theodore Roosevelt Award of the National Collegiate Athletic Association.
2007	➤	November 16, Eunice is honored with a tribute at the John F. Kennedy Presidential Library and Museum.

Learn More about Eunice Kennedy Shriver, Special Olympics, and Volunteerism

- Kennedy, Mike. *Special Olympics (True Books: Sports)*. Children's Press, 2003.
- Sabin, Ellen. *The Giving Book: Open The Door To A Lifetime Of Giving*. Watering Can, 2004.
- Shriver, Maria. *What's Wrong With Timmy?* Little, Brown and Company, 2001.
- Lewis, Barbara A. *The Kid's Guide to Service Projects: Over 500 Service Ideas for Young People Who Want to Make a Difference*. Free Spirit Publishing, 1995.

Websites:

- A short biography of Eunice Kennedy Shriver: http://www.jfklibrary.org/Historical + Resources/Biographies + and + Profiles/ Biographies/Eunice + Kennedy + Shriver.htm
- The Eunice Kennedy Shriver National Center for Community of Caring: http://www.communityofcaring.org/

Glossary

aquatics (uh KWAH tikss) Water sports.

Biafra (bee AH frah) A portion of the African country of Nigeria that claimed independence from 1967 – 1970. When Biafra tried to become independent war resulted and many people died of starvation.

commemorative (kuh MEM uh ruh tiv) An item like a coin or stamp, or an event organized to remember someone or something.

competition (KOM puh TISH uhn) A contest or sporting event.

intellectual disability (in tuh LEK choo uhl   DISS uh bil uh tee) A mental disability that causes a person to learn more slowly than most people.

juvenile delinquent (JOO vuh nile   di LING kwuhnt) A young person who breaks the law.

mission (MISH uhn) A special job or task.

politics (POL uh tiks) The activities of politicians and political parties.

tribute (TRIB yoot) Something done, given, or said to show thanks or respect.

—24—
Tenley Emma Albright:
Olympic Gold Medalist and Surgeon

by Kathleen W. Deady

Eleven-year old Tenley sat in a chair in her home. She held her 6 week-old cousin in her arms. Suddenly, she did not feel well.

"Could you please come over and hold her," she said to her mother. "I'm afraid that I'm going to drop her."

Within a few hours, Tenley lay in a hospital bed with a fever, **nausea,** and muscle pain. She was unable to use her legs, her back, or her neck. The **diagnosis** was **polio**. Tenley might never walk again.

· · · · ◌◌ · · · ·

Tenley Emma Albright was born in 1935 in Newton Center, Massachusetts. She was the only daughter of Hollis and Elin Albright. Her father was a well-known surgeon in Boston. Tenley and her younger brother Niles lived an **affluent** life.

At age 8, Tenley received her first pair of skates. Her parents made a skating rink in their yard. Before long, Tenley began taking lessons at the Skating Club of Boston.

Tenley loved skating. However, she thought the technical moves were boring. Her coach told her that if she ever wanted to compete, she would have to learn them. Tenley soon liked the **discipline** and focus that she needed to do them well. She began taking skating more seriously.

In the fall of 1946, Tenley became very ill with polio. The doctors feared she would be **paralyzed**. One day, the doctors said they would soon ask her to take three steps. All week, Tenley pictured herself walking and imagined what it would be like. On Friday, she did take a few steps. Slowly, she began to recover.

When Tenley finally went home, she was still very weak. Doctors urged her to try skating again to get stronger. It was very good advice. Four months later, she won her first major skating competition.

Over the next few years, Tenley continued to win. In 1952, she won the silver medal at the Olympics. She also won her first U.S. Championship.

In 1953, Tenley became the first American woman to win the World Figure Skating Championship. She then won the North American and the U.S. Championships. These three wins made Tenley the first triple-crown winner ever.

Skating was very important to Tenley. However, she also wanted to be a doctor. That fall, Tenley entered Radcliffe College. While attending classes, she continued to fit in seven hours of skating practice every day.

In 1955, Tenley took a break from school to train for the

TIDBITS

In 1946, polio was a dreaded disease. People knew very little about where it came from or how you could catch it. Doctors did not know how to treat the illness. People were often in the hospital for months, and many were left disabled. Today polio is very rare because we have a **vaccination** to prevent it.

◆•◆

Tenley's coach, Maribel Vinson Owen, was a former Olympic medalist herself. She quickly saw Tenley's talent and encouraged her.

TIDBITS

The technical moves, called **compulsory** figures, included a series of tight loops such as a figure eight. Skaters had to carve these forms in the ice with the edge of their skate blade.

◦•◦

While recovering from polio, Tenley fell a lot at first when she was skating. She later said, "If you don't fall down, you aren't trying hard enough."

◦•◦

The 1956 Olympics were the first winter Olympics to be shown on television around the world.

1956 Olympics. Two weeks before the competition, she fell. Her skate blade severely cut her right ankle. Few thought she would be able to compete, but Tenley had other ideas. Still in pain, Tenley became the first American woman ever to win a gold medal in figure skating.

Tenley retired from skating in 1957. She entered Harvard Medical School. She was one of only five women in the class. Four years later, she graduated and joined her father's medical practice Boston.

Tenley has had a very successful career in medicine. She has been a surgeon and a cancer researcher. She believes the discipline she learned as an athlete helped her succeed as a doctor.

But Tenley never forgot her first love, and has continued to skate throughout her life. "I always wanted to fly," she says, "and for me skating is the closest you can come to it."

Tenley Albright was one of only five women students in her class at Harvard Medical School.

Timeline: Tenley Emma Albright

1935	►	July 18, born to Hollis Albright, a well-known Boston surgeon, and Elin Albright in Newton Center, Massachusetts.
1946	►	Diagnosed with polio at age 11, hospitalized for three weeks.
		Four months later, wins **Eastern Juvenile Skating Championship.**
1949	►	At age 13, wins National Ladies Novice Singles Championship.
1950	►	Wins National Junior Championship.
1952	►	At age 16, wins silver medal in Winter Olympics in Oslo, Norway.
		Wins the U.S Women's Championship, the first of five U.S. titles in a row.
1953	►	First American woman to win World Figure Skating Championship.
		Also wins North American Championship, and second U.S. Championship.
		Enters Radcliffe College in Pre-Med program to become a doctor.
1954	►	Wins 3rd U.S. Women's Championship.
1955	►	Wins 4th U.S. Women's Championship.
		Takes leave from Radcliffe College after 2 years to train for 1956 Olympics.
1956	►	Wins gold medal in Winter Olympics at Cortina d'Ampezzo, Italy.
		Back at Radcliffe, finishes in three years.
1957	►	Retires from skating, enters Harvard Medical School.
1961	►	Graduates from Harvard Medical School, joins her father's medical practice in Boston.
1962	►	Marries Tudor Gardiner, they have three daughters Lilla Rhys, Elin, and Elee Emma.
1974	►	Is inducted into Ice Skating Hall of Fame.
1976	►	Is inducted into U.S. Figure Skating Hall of Fame.
1979	►	Becomes first woman to serve on U.S. Olympic Committee.
1981	►	Marries second husband, Gerald W. Blakeley, Jr.
1988	►	Is inducted into U.S Olympic Hall of Fame.
2000	►	Sports Illustrated names her one of the 100 Greatest Female Athletes.

Learn More About Tenley Albright, Olympic Skating, and Polio

- Freese, Joan. *Play-By-Play Figure Skating.* Lerner Sports, 2003.
- Hasday, Judy L. *Extraordinary Women Athletes*. Children's Press, 2000.
- Peters, Stephanie True. *Polio*. Marshall Cavendish Inc., 2005.

Websites:

- Academy of Achievement: Tenley Albright biography:
  http://www.achievement.org/autodoc/page/alb0bio-1
- Academy of Achievement: Tenley Albright interview:
  http://www.achievement.org/autodoc/page/alb0int-1
- Celebrating America's Women Physicians: Dr. Tenley E. Albright:
  http://www.nlm.nih.gov/changingthefaceofmedicine/physicians/biography_3.html
- Sports Illustrated for Women:
  http://sportsillustrated.cnn.com/siforwomen/top_100/47/

Glossary

affluent (AF loo UHNT) Well off, having enough money to live very comfortably.

compulsory (kuhm PUHL suh re) Something that must be done because of a rule or law.

diagnosis (dye uhg NOHSS uhss) The act of identifying a disease or illness based on a person's symptoms.

discipline (DISS uh plin) Control over the way a person or others behave.

Eastern Juvenile Skating Championship (EEST urn JOO vuh NILE SKAYT ing CHAM pee uhn ship) A skating competition for children under 12 years of age.

nausea (NAW zee uh) A feeling of being sick to your stomach.

paralyzed (PA ruh lized) To be unable to move, usually forever.

polio (POH lee oh) A serious and contagious viral disease. For many, it caused paralysis in their arms, legs, and lungs.

vaccination (vak suh NAY shun) An injection of medicine to prevent disease.

Laurie Stephens:
Paralympic
Alpine Skier

by Kathleen W. Deady

*F*ive-year-old Laurie climbed her slide and slid back down. She played tag and capture the flag with friends. She learned to dribble a basketball and shoot hoops. Before long, Laurie could swim the length of a pool faster than other children.

Many people thought Laurie could not accomplish things like other children. Why? Because she could not walk like them. But Laurie's parents wanted her to believe she *was*, in many ways, like other children. Her father always told her, "You can do everything, just a little different than I do." They wanted her to be independent.

But even Laurie's parents could not have imagined just how much she could do.

· · · · ᐰ · · · ·

Laurie Stephens was born on March 5, 1984 in Beverly, MA. She was born with a birth defect called **spina bifida**. This problem occurs when a

TIDBITS

In high school, Laurie joined a sports program called Northeast Passage. The coordinator said, "Laurie may be the most . . . self-driven athlete I have ever met, and that is regardless of ability."

◆—◆

Laurie still swims as part of her training for skiing.

◆—◆

Growing up, Laurie used leg braces and crutches. Her college campus was very large. After about two weeks, she switched to a wheelchair.

baby's spine does not grow properly before it is born. The baby may be partly or fully **paralyzed**. Laurie's legs are paralyzed. She uses braces with crutches or a wheelchair to get around.

Laurie never let her disability stop her from doing things. When she was five, her parents took her to a sports clinic. They saw she had a strong drive to compete. In every sport she tried, she was determined to do her best. Laurie soon entered **regional meets** in both swimming and wheelchair racing. At eight, Laurie competed at the national level.

When she was twelve, Laurie went with a group of disabled skiers to Loon Mountain in Lincoln, New Hampshire. She learned to sit-ski using a mono-ski, which looks like a chair on a single ski. Laurie discovered she loved skiing. Every weekend, her father drove her to Loon Mountain. Laurie would spend the whole day on the slopes, often the last off the chair lift at night.

"You really feel free and out of your disability," she says. "You can do what other able bodied skiers can do."

In 1998, Laurie started high school. She continued to compete in wheelchair racing and swimming. As a sophomore, she joined the New England Disabled Ski team. That year, Laurie skied in her first U.S. Nationals.

After graduating, Laurie entered the University of New Hampshire (UNH). She often traveled to train and compete. Laurie arranged with her professors to keep up with her classes. She sent them work on line, and made up anything she missed.

In 2004, Laurie joined the U.S. Disabled Olympic Ski Team. That year, she won all six **giant slalom** races on the World Cup

circuit. The next year, she wanted to prove that 2004 was not just a one-time thing. And prove it she did. Laurie won ten of her sixteen races.

In 2006, Laurie was the overall World Cup Champion for the third year. She also took time off from college to train for the **Paralympics**. Her hard work paid off with two gold medals and a silver.

Laurie continues to train, compete, and win. In 2007, she was World Cup **Super G** champion. She also graduated from college. After an injury, Laurie returned to training in 2008. She may return to school to continue her education. But for now, she is focused on skiing and winning.

Laurie once said after a win, "Now I just have to do it again." With such drive, she may well do it again and again. Could her parents have imagined such success?

Laurie races on a mono-ski—a kind of chair set on one ski.

TIDBITS

At UNH, Laurie studied **therapeutic recreation.** She wants to combine sports and working with disabled people.

•◆•

The Winter Paralympics started in Sweden in 1976.

•◆•

At the Paralympics, Laurie finished the Super G three seconds ahead of her competition.

•◆•

Of skiing, Laurie says, "I'm going to keep doing it as long as I'm having fun."

•◆•

Laurie loves movies, pasta, and punk rock music.

Timeline: Laurie Stephens

1984	➤	March 5, born in Beverly, Massachusetts to John Stephens and Donna Bettencourt Stephens, first of two children. Grows up in Wenham.
1987	➤	May 12, brother Scott born.
1989	➤	Starts going to sports clinic at the Massachusetts Hospital School for children with Spina Bifida in Canton, MA.
1992	➤	Competes at the national level in swimming and wheelchair racing.
1993	➤	Tries 4-track skiing, standing up using 2 skis and two hand held **outriggers**.
1996	➤	Starts mono-skiing at Loon Mountain in NH.
1998	➤	Enters Hamilton-Wenham Regional High School in Wenham, Massachusetts.
1999–2000	➤	Sets U.S. records in disabled swimming for 100 meter and 200 meter backstroke.
		Joins New England Disabled Ski Team.
2002	➤	Graduates from high school, enters UNH, studies therapeutic recreation.
2003	➤	U.S. Downhill Ski Champion, named to U.S. Disabled Ski Team (USDST) for 2004.
2004	➤	U.S. Downhill and Super G Champion.
		Mono-ski Overall Champion.
		World Championship Giant Slalom Silver medalist.
2005	➤	January, wins first ever mono-ski event at Winter X-Games in Aspen Colorado; World Cup, wins all disabled titles in Mono-Skiing, Named Paralympian of the Year by the U.S. Olympic Committee.
2006	➤	World Cup, wins Super G and Giant Slalom; Mono-ski Overall Champion for third year; National Champion in Downhill, Super G, Giant Slalom and Slalom;
		March, competes at Paralympics in Turin, Italy. Wins gold medal in woman's sitting Super G and Downhill, Silver medal in Giant Slalom.
		ESPY Nomination for best Female Athlete with a Disability.
		Women's Sports Foundation nomination for Sportswoman of the Year.
2007	➤	World Cup: Wins Super G.
		December, graduates from University of New Hampshire.
2008	➤	Injury prevents competing in 2008 World Cup; returns to training in spring.

Learn More About Laurie, Spina Bifida, and the Paralympics

- Kent, Deborah. ***Athletes with Disabilities***. Franklin Watts, 2003.
- Watson, Stephanie. ***Spina Bifida*** (Genetic and Developmental Diseases and Disorders). Rosen Publishing, September, 2008.

Websites:

- Biography on Laurie:
  http://groupbenefits.thehartford.com/usp/bios/stephens.htl
- Laurie's Website:
  http://www.turnerresourcemail.com/

Glossary

circuit (SUR kit) A circular route. In sports, a group of competitions.

Giant Slalom (JYE uhnt SLAH luhm) An athletic event in which competitors ski downhill, zigzagging between gates.

outrigger (OUT rig ur) Kind of frame held by a skier on either side, to keep the skier from falling.

Paralympics (PA rah limp ikss) International Olympics held every four years in which the competitors have some sort of physical disability and use modified equipment.

paralyzed (PA ruh lized) Losing the power to feel or move part of the body.

regional meet (REE juhn uhl MEET) Competition between teams located in the same region or area.

spina bifida (SPEYE nuh bif i duh) A birth defect affecting a person's spine.

Super G (SOO pur JEE) A downhill skiing race that has fewer gates set farther apart than those used in a giant slalom over a longer course and with higher speeds. Also called Super Giant Slalom.

therapeutic recreation (THER uh pyoo tik rek ree AY shuhn) Providing treatment and activities such as arts and crafts, sports, dance, music, and drama for people with disabilities or illnesses to help them maintain their physical, mental, and emotional well-being.

Research, Interviews, and Special Thanks _____

Additional research conducted at:
- The Rebecca Nurse Homestead
- The Porter-Phelps-Huntington House
- Orchard House at Concord, MA
- Houghton Library at Harvard University

Interview conducted with:
- Laurie Stephens

Special thanks to:
- Matthew Bose, research librarian, from the Oak Bluffs Public Library, Oak Bluffs, MA for information about Nancy Harkness Love.

- Helen and Stephen Chen for generously sharing information about their mother.

- Susan Lisk at Forty Acres in Hadley, MA (the Porter-Phelps-Huntington House).

- Chip Baker for taking time out of a very stressful day to give a personal tour of the Porter-Phelps-Huntington House.

- Jan Turnquist, Executive Director of Orchard House

- Sheila Brown, Photo Researcher

A complete research bibliography for *Women of the Bay State : 25 Massachusetts Women You Should Know* is available in a downloadable PDF format from Apprentice Shop Books, LLC at www.apprenticeshopbooks.com

Partial Research Bibliography—Women of the Bay State*

CHAPTER 1: Mary Dyer: *Quaker Martyr*

Hill Lindley, Susan. *You Have Stept Out of Your Place: a History of Women and Religion in America*. Louisville, KY: Westminster John Knox P, 1996. 8-22.

"Quaker Mary Dyer." *The Official Website of the Commonwealth of Massachusetts*. 2008. Commonwealth of Massachusetts. 4 Apr. 2008 < http://www/mass/gov/?pageID = mg2termin al&L = 6&L0 = Home&L1 > .

Rogers, Horatia. *Mary Dyer: the Quaker Martyr*. Providence, Rhode Island: Preston and Rounds, 1896.

Shriver, George, ed. *Dictionary of Heresy Trials in American Christianity*. Westport, Connecticut: Greenwood P, 1997. 120-128.

CHAPTER 2: Anne Dudley Bradstreet: *America's First Poet*

"Anne Bradstreet Biography." 22 Oct. 2002. 6 June 2008 < http://www.annebradstreet.com/anne_bradstreet_ bio_001.htm > .

"Anne Bradstreet 1612 - 1672." *Poets of Cambridge, U.S.A.* Harvard Square Library. 13 June 2008 < http://www. harvardsquarelibrary.org/poets/bradstreet.php > .

"April 7 1630: Puritans Leave for Massachusetts." *Mass Moments*. Massachusetts Foundation for the Humanities. 13 June 2008 < http://www.massmoments.org/moment. cfm?mid = 106 > .

Behling, Susanne "Sam" "Anne Dudley Bradstreet." *Notable Women Ancestors*. 6 June 2008 < http://www.rootsweb. ancestry.com/ ~ nwa/bradstreet.html > .

"Colonial America Massachusetts Bay Colony 1630." *Online Highway-Travel and History*. 13 June 2008 < http://www.u-s-history.com/pages/h572.html > .

CHAPTER 3: Rebecca Towne Nurse: *The Salem Witch Trials*

Norton, Mary Beth. **In the Devil's Snare: The Salem Witchcraft Crisis of 1692**. Knopf, 2002.

Ray, Benjamin, ed. *Salem Witch Trials: Documentary Archive and Transcription Project*. 2002. University of Virginia. 10 Oct. 2008 < http://etext.lib.virginia.edu/salem/witchcraft/ > .

Roach, Marilynne K. **The Salem Witch Trials: A Day-by-Day Chronicle of a Community Under Siege**. Taylor Trade Publishing, 2004.

Rosenthal, Bernard. **Salem Story: Reading the Witch Trials of 1692** *(Cambridge Studies in American Literature and Culture)* Cambridge University Press, 1995.

CHAPTER 4: Abigail Adams: *First Lady of the United States*

"Abigail Smith Adams." The Massachusetts Historical Society. 30 Aug. 2008 < http://www.masshist.org/adams/biographical. cfm > .

"Abigail Smith Adams." *The White House*. The White House. 30 Aug. 2008 < http://www.whitehouse.gov/history/firstladies/ aa2.html > .

Akers, Charles W. *Abigail Adams: An American Woman*. Boston, MA: Little, Brown and Company, 1980.

"Bunker Hill Exhibit." 2003. The Massachusetts Historical Society. 30 Aug. 2008 < http://www.masshist.org/bh/ aadamsbio.html > .

"First Lady Biography: Abigail Adams." 2005. The National First Ladies Library. 30 Aug. 2008 < http://www.firstladies.org/ biographies/firstladies.aspx?biography = 2 > .

Hogan, Margaret A., and C. James Taylor, eds. *My Dearest Friend: Letters of Abigail and John Adams*. Cambridge, MA: The Belknap P of Harvard UP, 2007.

CHAPTER 5: Elizabeth Porter Phelps: *Diary Keeper*

Carlisle, Elizabeth Pendergast. *Earthbound and Heavenbent : Elizabeth Porter Phelps and Life at Forty Acres (1747-1817)*. New York: Scribner, 2007.

Clark, Christopher. *The Roots of Rural Capitalism : Western Massachusetts, 1780-1860*. New York: Cornell UP, 1992.

Huntington, James Lincoln. *Forty Acres*. New York, NY: Hastings House, 1949.

Miller, Marla R. *The Needle's Eye : Women and Work in the Age of Revolution*. New York: University of Massachusetts P, 2006.

Nylander, Jane C. *Our Own Snug Fireside : Images of the New England Home, 1760-1860*. New York: Yale UP, 1994.

Ulrich, Laurel T. "Housewife and Gadder: Themes of Self-Sufficiency and Community in Eighteenth-Century New England." *Families in the U.S. : Kinship and Domestic Politics*. Ed. Karen V. Hansen and Anita I. Garey. New York: Temple UP, 1998. 241 + . Google Books.

CHAPTER 6: Lucretia Coffin Mott: *Suffragette and Abolitionist*

Bryant, Jennifer Fisher. *Lucretia Mott: a Guiding Light*. Grand Rapids, Michigan: William B. Eerdmans Company, 1996.

Hill, Susan Lindley. *You Have Stept Out of Your Place: a History of Women and Religion in America*. Louisville, KY: Westminster John Knox, 1996.

Hope Bacon, Margaret. *Valiant Friend: the Life of Lucretia Mott*. New York, New York: Walker and Company, 1980.

"Living the Legacy: the Women's Rights Movement 1848-1998." May-June < http://www.legacy98.org/move-hist.html > .

"Lucretia Coffin Mott." *American National Biography Online*. Oxford Companion of American History. May-June 2008 < http://www.anb.org/articles/15/15-00494.html > .

Wilson Palmer, Beverly, ed. "Lucretia Coffin Mott Chronology." *Lucretia Coffin Mott Papers Project*. May 2008 < http://www. mott.pomona.edu > .

"Women of the Hall: Lucretia Mott." *National Women's Hall of Fame*. May-June 2008 < http://www.greatwomen.org/ women.php?action = viewone&id = 112 > .

CHAPTER 7: Dorothea Dix: *Friend of the Friendless*

Book Review: *Dorothea Lynde Dix, Philanthropist. New York Times* 20 Oct. 1890. New York Times Archive. 8 June 2008. Keyword: Dorothea Dix.

Brown, Thomas J. *Dorothea Dix Vol. 127 : New England Reformer*. New York: Harvard UP, 1998.

continued Partial Research Bibliography—Women of the Bay State*

Dix, Dorothea L. *On Behalf of the Insane Poor : Selected Reports, 1843-1852.* Boston: Ayer Company, Incorporated, 1975.

Dix, Dorothea L. *Remarks on Prisons and Prison Discipline in the United States.* Joseph Kite, 1845. 17 Oct. 2005. Google Books. 15 Oct. 2008. Keyword: Dorothea Lynde Dix.

Gollaher, David. *Voice for the Mad : A Life of Dorothea Dix.* New York: Free P, 1995. 24 Aug. 2007. Google Books. 15 Oct. 2008. Keyword: Dorothea Dix.

CHAPTER 8: Maria Mitchell: *Astronomer and Educator*

Daniels, Elizabeth A. "Maria Mitchell and Women's Rights." *Vassar Encyclopedia.* 2004. Vassar College. 8 Apr. 2008 < http://vcencyclopedia.vassar.edu/index.php/Maria_Mitchell_and_Women%27s_Rights > .

Daniels, Elizabeth A. "Maria Mitchell Observatory." *Vassar Encyclopedia.* 2004. Vassar College. 8 Apr. 2008 < http://vcencyclopedia.vassar.edu/index.php/Maria_Mitchell_Observatory > .

Daniels, Elizabeth A. "Maria Mitchell." *Vassar Encyclopedia.* 2004. Vassar College. 8 Apr. 2008 < http://vcencyclopedia.vassar.edu/index.php/Maria_Mitchell > .

Kendall, Phebe M., comp. *Maria Mitchell: Life, Letters, and Journals.* Boston: Lee and Shepard, 1896. 02 Apr. 2008 < http://sdr.lib.umich.edu/cgi/pt?id = mdp.39015033356646 > .

Macdonald, JoAnn. "Maria Mitchell." *Dictionary of Unitarian and Universalist Biography.* 2008. Unitarian Universalist Historical Society. 30 Mar. 2008 < http://www25.uua.org/uuhs/duub/articles/mariamitchell.html > .

CHAPTER 9: Lucy Larcom: *Millgirl, Teacher, Poet*

Larcom, Jen. "Lucy Larcom." *Larcom Family Tree.* 2006. 11 June 2008 < http://www.larcomfamilytree.com/lucy/index.html > .

Larcom, Lucy. *A New England Girlhood Outlined from Memory.* Boston: Houghton Mifflin Company, 1889.

"Lucy Larcom 1824-1893." *The American Civil War: Letters and Diaries.* 2001. University of Chicago. 11 June 2008 < http://www.alexanderstreet2.com/cwldlive/bios/a40bio.html > .

Marchalonis, Shirley, Heidi L. Jacobs, and Jennifer Putzi. "Lucy Larcom Biography." *Dictionary of Literary Biography.* 2005-2006. Thomson Gale, a part of the Thomson Corporation. 25 July 2008 < http://www.bookrags.com/biography/lucy-larcom-dlb/ > .

Marchalonis, Shirley. *The Worlds of Lucy Larcom 1824-1893.* Athens, Georgia: The University of Georgia Press, 1989.

CHAPTER 10: Louisa May Alcott: *Writer, Reformer, Celebrity*

Eiselein, Gregory K., and Anne Phillips, eds. *The Louisa May Alcott Encyclopedia.* New York: Greenwood P, 2001. Includes several articles by this author.

Extraordinary Women : Lousia May Alcott: Life, Letters and Journals. New York, NY: Random House Value, 2005. Various editions of Louisa's journals are available.

Johnston, Norma. *Louisa May : The World and Works of Louisa May Alcott.* New York: Simon & Schuster Children's, 1991.

Published for the young reader but with solid scholarship and documentation.

Matteson, John. *Eden's Outcasts: The Story of Louisa May Alcott and Her Father.* W.W. Norton, 2007. Booklist starred review.

Shealy, Daniel, ed. *Alcott in Her Own Time : A Biographical Chronicle of Her Life, Drawn from Recollections, Interviews, and Memoirs by Family, Friends, and Associates.* New York: University of Iowa P, 2005. A fascinating collection.

CHAPTER 11: Isabella Stuart Gardner: *Patron of the Arts*

Hall, Alexandra. "The New Brahmins." *Boston Magazine* May 2004. *Boston: The Best of Boston Everyday.* Boston Magazine. < http://www.bostonmagazine.com/articles/the_new_brahmins/ > .

"Isabella Stewart Gardner, 1840-1924." *The Correspondence of James McNeill Whistler.* University of Glasgow. < http://www.whistler.arts.gla.ac.uk/biog/gard_is.htm > .

Isabella Stewart Gardner Museum. "Boston's Original Rowdy Red Sox Fan." Press release. 24 Oct. 2007. Isabella Stewart Gardner Museum. < http://www.gardnermuseum.org/press_releases/2007/redsox_worldseries_release.pdf > .

"The Museum: Isabella Stewart Gardner." *Isabella Stewart Gardner Museum.* Isabella Stewart Gardner Museum. < http://www.gardnermuseum.org/the_museum/isabella.asp > .

CHAPTER 12: Edith Swallow Richards: *First Woman Chemist*

"Ellen Swallow Richards." *Chemical Achievers: The Human Face of Chemical Sciences.* Chemical Heritage Foundation. 24 Apr. 2008 < http://www.chemheritage.org/classroom/chemach/environment/richards.html > .

"Ellen Swallow Richards (1842-1911)." *Women of the Hall.* National Women's Hall of Fame. 24 Apr. 2008 < http://www.greatwomen.org/women.php?action = viewone&id = 123 > .

Hunt, Caroline L. *The Life of Ellen H. Richards.* Boston, MA: Whitcomb & Hunt, 1912.

Kovarik, Bill. "Ellen Swallow Richards and the Progressive Women's Reform Movement." *Environmental History Timeline.* Radford University. 24 Apr. 2008 < http://www.runet.edu/ ~ wkovarik/envhist/richards.html > .

"Massachusetts Institute of Technology: Women's Laboratory, 1876-1883." Aug. 1999. Massachusetts Institute of Technology. 24 Apr. 2008 < http://libraries.mit.edu/archives/exhibits/esr/esr-womenslab.html > .

Swallow Richards, Ellen. "The Rumford Kitchen: Exhibit at World's Columbian Exposition, Chicago, 1893." Massachusetts Institute of Technology. 24 Apr. 2008 < http://libraries.mit.edu/archives/exhibits/esr/esr-rumford.html > .

CHAPTER 13: Mary Mahoney: *First Black Professional Nurse*

Carnegie, Mary Elizabeth. The Path We Tread: Blacks in Nursing, 1854-1994. 3rd ed. New York: National League of Nursing P, 1995.

* A complete research bibliography is available in downloadable PDF format from www.apprenticeshopbooks.com

Chayer, Mary Ella. "Mary Eliza Mahoney." The American Journal of Nursing Apr. 1954: 429-431.

Darraj, Susan M. Mary Eliza Mahoney and the Legacy of African-American Nurses. Philadelphia, PA: Chelsea House, 2005.

Davis, Althea T. Early Black American Leaders in Nursing: Architects for Integration and Equality. Boston: Jones & Bartlett, 1999.

Doona, Mary Ellen. ""Gravesite of Mary E. Mahoney." American Association for the History of Nursing. 21 Oct. 2005. 31 May 2008 < http://www.aahn.org/gravesites/mahoney.html > .

CHAPTER 14: Edith Wharton: *Writer*

Benstock, Shari. *No Gifts From Chazznce*. New York,, NY: Charles Scribner's Sons, 1994.

Dwight, Eleanor, and Viola Hopkins Winner. "Edith Wharton's World." National Portrait Gallery. 02 Aug. 2008 < http://npg.sci.edu/exh/wharton/whar3.htm > .

"Edith Wharton: Life Stories, Books and Links." 02 Aug. 2008 < http://www.today in literature.com/biography/edith.wharton.asp#stories > .

"Edith Wharton." *Domestic Goddess*. 14 July 1998. 02 Aug. 2008 < http://www.womenwriters.net/domesticgoddess/wharton1.htm > .

Lee, Hermione. *Edith Wharton*. New York, NY: Alfred A. Knopf, 2007.

CHAPTER 15: Florence Bascom: *Geologist*

James, Edward T., ed. *Notable American Women 1607-1915: a Biographical Dictionary*. Vol. I. Cambridge, MA: Belknap P of Harvard U. P, 1971. 108-110.

Knopf, Eleanora B. "Memorial of Florence Bascom." *American Mineralogist* 31 (1946): 168-172.

Ogilvie, Ida H. "Obituary: Florence Bascom 1862-1945." *Science* 28 Sept. 1945: 320-321.

Smith, Isabel F. *The Stone Lady: a Memoir of Florence Bascom*. Bryn Mawr, PA: Bryn Mawr College, 1981.

CHAPTER 16: Edith Norse Rogers: *A Life in Congress*

"Born of Controversy: The GI Bill of Rights." *GI Bill Website*. U.S. Department of Veterans Affairs. 14 Oct. 2008 < http://www.gibill.va.gov/gi_bill_info/history.htm > .

Brown, Dorothy M. "Rogers, Edith Nourse." *American National Biography*. Ed. John A. Garraty and Mark C. Carnes. Vol. 8. New York: Oxford U. Pr., 1999. 752-53.

Committee on House Administration, House (U.S.). "Edith Nourse Rogers 1881-1960." *Women in Congress 1917-2006*. Washington D.C.: U.S. G.P.O., 2006. 70-75.

"Congressman and Mrs. Rogers on Ship Attacked by U-Boat--Warned of Air Raid." *Lowell Sun* 30 Oct. 1917: 1.

"Edith Nourse Rogers." *Fort Devens Museum*. Fort Devens Museum. 14 Oct. 2008 < http://www.fortdevensmuseum.org/edithnourserogers.htm > .

CHAPTER 17: Marita Bonner: *Harlem Renaissance Writer*

The African American Registry. < http://www.aaregistry.com/african_history/975/marita_bonner_creator_of_frye > .

Alston et al, Joseph. "Marita Odette Bonner." *VG: Artist Biography: Marita Odette*. Jan. 2003. University of Minnesota. 24 Apr. 2008 < http://voices.cla.umn.edu/vg/bios/entries/bonner_marita_odette.html > .

Cooper, Anna J. "On Being Young--a Woman--and Colored." *Negro History Bulletin* (1996): 36 + . 24 July 2008.

Flynn, Jocye. "Marita Bonner Occomy." *Dictionary of Literary Biography*. Thomson Gale, 2005-2006.

Johnson Lewis, Jone. "Marita Bonner." *About.com Women's History*. 24 Apr. 2008 < http://womenshistory.about.com/od/harlemrenaissance/p/marita_bonner.htm > .

Joyce, Flynn, and Joyce O. Stricklin. *Frye Street and Environs: The Collected Works of Marita Bonner*. Boston, MA: Beacon, 1987.

CHAPTER 18: Katharine Lane Weems: *Sculptor*

Ambler, Louise T. *Katharine Lane Weems: Sculpture and Drawings*. Boston: The Boston Atheneum, 1987.

Greenthal, Kathryn, Paula M. Kozol, and Jan S. Ramirez. *American Figurative Sculpture in the Museum of Fine Arts, Boston*. New York: Museum of Fine Arts, Boston, 1986.

"Katharine (Lane) Weems, a sculptor who specialized in animal studies, died Saturday in her Back Bay home. She was 89." *Boston Globe* 15 Feb. 1989.

"Lyman Library: Weems Animal Sculptures Audio Slideshow." *Museum of Science*. Museum of Science, Boston. 15 Oct. 2008 < http://http://www.mos.org/events_activities/lyman_library&d = 1819 > .

Weems, Katherine L., and Edward Weeks. *Odds Were Against Me: A Memoir*. New York: Vantage, 1985.

Weems, Katherine L. *Katharine Lane Weems papers, 1865-1989* (microfilm reel 724). Washington D.C.: Archives of American Art.

CHAPTER 19: Betty Davis: *Actress*

"Bette Davis." *IMDb The Internet Movie Data Base*. 11 Aug. 2008 < http://www.imd.com/name/nm0000012/ > .

Bette Davis: The Official Website. 11 Aug. 2008 < http://www.bettedavis.com > .

"Bette Davis." *The Quotations Page*. 11 Aug. 2008 < http://www.quotationspage.com/quotes/bette_davis/ > .

Chandler, Charlotte. *The Girl Who Walked Home Alone*. New York: Simon and Schuster, 2006.

Davis, Bette, With Michael Herskowitz. *This 'N That*. New York: G. P. Putnam's Sons, 1987.

Emerson, Jim. "Meeting Miss Davis." 11 Aug. 2008 < http://www.cinepad.com/bettedavis.htm > .

CHAPTER 20: Mary "Polly" Ingraham Bunting: *Scientist and Reformer*

Moot O'Hern, Elizabeth. *Profiles of Pioneer Women Scientists*. Washington, DC: Acropolis Books Ltd., 1985.

"One Woman, Two Lives." *Time Magazine* 03 Nov. 1961. 3 July 2008. Keyword: Mary Bunting. < http://www.time.com/ time/magazine/article/0,9171,897907,00.html > .

President and Fellows of Harvard College. "History of the Fellowship Program." *Radcliffe Institute for Advanced Study Harvard University.* 2008. Harvard University. 3 July 2008 < www.Radcliffe.edu/print/fellowships/history.htm > .

"Togetherness in Cambridge." *Time Magazine* 30 May 1960. 3 July 2008. Keyword: Mary Bunting. < http://www.time.com/ time/magazine/article/0,9171,939685-2,00.html > .

Yaffe, Elaine. *Mary Ingraham Bunting: Her Two Lives.* Savannnah: Frederic C. Beil, 2005.

CHAPTER 21: Nancy Harkness Love: *First Woman to Fly for the Military*

"The American Experience: Nancy Harkness Love." *PBS.org.* < http://www.pbs.org/wgbh/amex/flygirls/peopleevents/ pandeamex03.html > .

Cole, Wendy. *Women Pilots of World War II.* Salt Lake City: University of Utah P, 2002.

Douglas, Deborah G. "Nancy Harkness Love." *Historynet.com.* < http://www.historynet.com/nancy-harkness-love-female-pilot-and-first-to-fly-for-the-us-military.htm > .

"Nancy Harkness Love." *Davis Monthan Aviation Field Register.* 2008. < http://www.dmairfield.org/people/harkness_nl/ index.html > .

Parrish, Deanie. "Nancy Harkness Love." *Wings Across America.* 2005. < http://www.wingsacrossamerica.us/wasp/bio_love. htm > .

CHAPTER 22: Joyce Chen: *Chef*

Chen, Helen. *Helen Chen's Chinese Home Cooking.* New York, NY: Hearst Books, 1994.

Chen, Joyce. *Joyce Chen Cook Book.* Philadelphia, PA: J.B. Lippincott Co., 1962.

"Correspondence with Helen and Stephen Chen, children of Joyce Chen." E-mail to the author. Aug. 2008.

"For Some, Thanksgiving Meant Turkey and Peking Ravioli: The Holiday Celebration was Spiced with Variety." *Boston Globe* 27 Nov. 1981.

Haag, John. "Joyce Chen." *Women in World History: A Biographical Encyclopedia.* Ed. Anne Commire. Vol. 3. Waterford, CT: Yorkin Publications, 1994. 662-64.

CHAPTER 23: Eunice Kennedy Shriver: *Founder of the Special Olympics*

"Eunice Kennedy Shriver, Doctor of Public Service." *The Shriver Center.* < http://www.shrivercenter.org/about_ekshriver. html > .

"Historical Resources: Biographies and Profiles, Eunice Kennedy Shriver." *John F. Kennedy Presidential Library and Museum.* < http://www.jfklibrary.org/historical + resources/ biographies + and + profiles/biographies/ eunice + kennedy + shriver.htm > .

Kirk, Jr., Paul G., Mary Ann Glendon, Maria Shriver, Mark Shriver, Robert Shriver, Anthony Shriver, Edward M. Kennedy, and Eunice Shriver. "A Tribute to Eunice

Kennedy Shriver." Kennedy Library Forums. The John F. Kennedy Presidential Library and Museum, Boston, MA. 16 Nov. 2007. *C-Span.* C-Span. < http://inside.c-spanarchives org:8080/cspan/cspan..csp?command = dprogram &record = 537139339 > .

Leamer, Laurence. *The Kennedy Women : The Saga of an American Family.* New York: Ballantine Books, 1996.

CHAPTER 24: Tenley Albright: *Olympic Gold Medalist and Surgeon*

"Biography: Dr. Tenley E. Albright." *National Library of Medicine.* 6 Aug. 2004. 30 Mar. 2008 < http://www.nlm. nih.gov/changingthefaceofmedicine/ > .

Hickok, Ralph. *A Who's Who of Sports Champions: Their Stories and Records.* Boston: Houghton Mifflin Company, 1995. 9.

"I Always Liked to Fly." *Newsweek.Com.* 26 Apr. 2005. Newsweek, Inc. 30 Mar. 2008 < http://www.newsweek. com/id/49388 > .

Long, Anna T. "Tenley E. Albright '57 Olympian, Surgeon, Teacher." *News: the Harvard Crimson Online Edition.* 01 June 2007. The Harvard Crimson, Inc. 30 Mar. 2008 < http://www.thecrimson.com/article.aspx?ref = 519035 > .

Oglesby, Carole A., Doreen L. Greenberg, Ruth L. Hall, Karen L. Hill, Frances Johnson, and Sheila E. Ridley, eds. "Tenley Albright." *Encyclopedia of Women and Sports in America.* Phoenix: Oryx P, 1998.

"Tenley Albright, Figure Skating." *Sports Illustrated for Women.* 2000. CNN/Sports Illustrated. 30 Mar. 2008 < http:// sportsillustrated.cnn.com/siforwomen/top_100/47/ > .

"Tenley Albright, Figure Skating." *Sports Illustrated for Women.* 2000. CNN/Sports Illustrated. 30 Mar. 2008 < http:// sportsillustrated.cnn.com/siforwomen/top_100/47/ > .

CHAPTER 25: Laurie Stephens: *Paralympic Alpine Skier*

"Biography: Laurie Stephens." *The Official Site of the US Ski Team.* 2008. United States Ski and Snowboard Association. 02 Aug. 2008 < http://www.usskiteam.com/public/team. php?sn = 2&did = 5&aid = 161 > .

Burnett, Carl. "Interview with Laurie." *No Two Are Alike.* 26 Apr. 2006. 18 Aug. 2008 < http://notwoarealike.blogspot. com/2006_04_01_archive.html > .

Clark, Danielle. "UNH senior medals in 2006 Paralympics." *The New Hampshire: The Student Publication of the University of New Hampshire.* 24 Mar. 2006. University of New Hampshire. < http://media.www.tnhonline.com/media/ storage/paper674/news/2006/03/24/news/unh-senior. medals.in.2006.paralympics-1715499.shtml > .

"Explore the Possibilities: Athletic Development." *Northeast Passage.* 2003-2007. University of New Hampshire. Aug. 2008 < http://www.nepassage.org/paralympic.html > .

Gosling, Nicholas. "Comfortable in the Fast Lane." *UNH Magazine Online.* Winter 2006. University of New Hampshire Alumni Association. 06 Aug. 2008 < http:// unhmagazine.unh.edu/w06/fastlane.html > .

* A complete research bibliography is available in downloadable PDF format from www.apprenticeshopbooks.com